A profound story about a young ma  the face of much adversity. For those addictions of any kind, Patrick's story proves that there is always help available. What is needed is the courage to seek it out. Despite setbacks along the way, Patrick found a pathway that led him back to his native village, his beloved donkeys, and true contentment. A most uplifting read.

PHILIP EGAN, nationally recognized Irish poet; author of *A Verseman's Harvest*

Donkeys have a reputation in popular culture as stubborn beasts. But as *Sanctuary* reveals, they can also be faithful friends— the very best kind of friend that is willing to carry a broken, traumatized man to a place of healing. Patrick Barrett's story begins in his family's Irish donkey sanctuary and invites us on his journey far from that place of safety and into a life marked by PTSD and addiction. However, that dark, distant place wasn't Barrett's final destination. *Sanctuary's* warmhearted, hopeful narrative is a reminder that there is always a way home—for each one of us.

MICHELLE VAN LOON, author of *Born to Wander: Recovering the Value of Our Pilgrim Identity*

From a man who had the good fortune to grow up in a sanctuary of donkeys, here's a true story as surefooted and mystical as the equines in his life. Shaped by his home village in Ireland, a strong family, and the deep friendships of rescued donkeys, Patrick Barrett leaves home to discover the world in all its beauty, sadness, and complexities. Only when he comes full circle—back to the sanctuary of steadfast donkeys—will he find what's missing inside. Patrick Barrett and Susy Flory offer a magical and yet very real story of one man's journey and the miracles that present themselves along the way. If you've known a donkey, you'll want to read this book. And if you've never known a donkey, you'll want to find one after you read this book—a warm and victorious story full of second chances for both human and beast.

CALLIE SMITH GRANT, editor of *Second-Chance Cats, The Horse of My Dreams,* and *Second-Chance Dogs;* winner of Dog Writers of America's Maxwell Award

What a beautiful thing to watch God use such downtrodden, disabused animals as donkeys to help restore and redeem a human soul. Patrick Barrett's story is inspiring, yearning, uplifting, hopeful, and right on time for our broken, hurting world.

PATRICIA RAYBON, author of *My First White Friend: Confessions on Race, Love, and Forgiveness* and *I Told the Mountain to Move: Learning to Pray So Things Change*

Sanctuary is a book for anyone longing to be inspired, whose soul craves being seen, or who needs a reminder that redemption is possible—no matter your situation. Reading this book felt like taking a walk through the hills of southern Ireland with Patrick Barrett and the rescue donkeys who helped him find his way home. Full of personal stories—some heartwarming, some heartbreaking, each a testimony to the power of redemption—*Sanctuary* is a must-read for any fan of memoir.

JENNIFER MARSHALL BLEAKLEY, author of *Joey: How a Blind Rescue Horse Helped Others Learn to See,* and *Pawverbs: 100 Inspirations to Delight an Animal Lover's Heart*

Sanctuary spoke to me on many levels. This is a story about healing, becoming part of a herd, and returning to a literal and spiritual rock that held a place for this sensitive soul, all along. I found the spiritual content compelling and gently told; this is an exquisite and deeply honest spiritual memoir. Highly recommended!

JENNIFER GRANT, author of *Dimming the Day*

"Who rescued who?" Those of us who have rescued animals know how true this bumper-sticker sentiment is! And indeed, Patrick Barrett's story of how rescue donkeys "led him home" speaks beautifully to how rescue and redemption work in this world. *Sanctuary* is a marvelous, hope-giving work, perfect for those invested in animal rescue and those who need to be reminded that God is in the rescue and redemption business.

CARYN RIVADENEIRA, author of the Helper Hounds series and the forthcoming *Saints of Feather & Fang: How the Animals We Love and Fear Connect Us to God*

As a survivor of medical trauma, I know firsthand the terrifying grip of PTSD and the powerful and surprising comfort an intuitive animal can provide. From the first page, *Sanctuary* captivated me with the beauty of the Irish landscape, Patrick's heartbreaking and hope-filled journey, and the steadfast wisdom of donkeys and their herds all along the way. Best of all, I was reminded of the truth that likewise healed me: We are never alone.

MICHELE CUSHATT, author of *Relentless: The Unshakeable Presence of a God Who Never Leaves*

Patrick Barrett had an uncanny connection with the donkeys that his family rescued. But who would ever predict how those donkeys would ultimately help rescue *him*? Set in the lush, mystical green hills of Ireland, *Sanctuary* is a poignant story of addiction, recovery, community, the hope we find in the sanctuary of God's love, and the animals and people who walk beside us.

KERI WYATT KENT, founder of A Powerful Story; author of *GodSpace: Embracing the Inconvenient Adventure of Intimacy with God*

My first impulse when reading *Sanctuary* was to find and snuggle a donkey foal, much like the one who appears in the opening and at the close of this excellent book. My second—and more significant—impulse was to feel wonder at God's great gifts: the gift of animals' healing ability but also of redemption, grace, and love. Patrick Barrett's lively (and lovely) story bears witness to the powerful presence of God's abundant love in the most unlikely places, including the Donkey Sanctuary Ireland where Barrett calls home.

MELANIE SPRINGER MOCK, professor of English at George Fox University, Newberg, Oregon; author of *Worthy: Finding Yourself in a World Expecting Someone Else*

Sanctuary is a multifaceted love story. It's a tale of the restorative connection between a sensitive, stubborn man and the equally intuitive, willful donkeys in his life. It's a drama that spotlights the redemptive grace of God and the rejuvenated life possible when a lost soul finds refuge in him. And it's a testimony to the tenacity of praying parents who never ever give up.

CHERI GREGORY, coauthor of *Sensitive & Strong: A Guide for Highly Sensitive Persons and Those Who Love Them*

Against a backdrop of misty emerald hills and sacred stone walls is a true story of a restless wanderer struggling to find peace in the midst of brokenness. For Patrick Barrett, taking in donkeys that were abandoned, abused, and neglected was part of his

Irish heritage for as long as he could remember. His connection ran deeper than changing straw or binding up wounds; he understood how it felt to be a misfit and wrestle with knowing who you really are. Brilliantly written and engaging from the first page to the last, *Sanctuary* speaks to anyone who has ever lost their way and found that the road they hoped would lead to a place of belonging is sometimes the one that leads back home.

MARCI SEITHER, creative storyteller

You don't have to like donkeys in order to fall in love with this heart-wrenching, heartwarming, and hope-filled book. Only an Irishman could make a tale so painful and harrowing such an utter delight. I especially recommend *Sanctuary* to anyone who loves and is praying for a prodigal. Patrick Barrett's miraculous and redemptive story will give you hope that no one is ever too far away from God's rescue and home.

ALISON HODGSON, author of *The Pug List: A Ridiculous Little Dog, a Family Who Lost Everything, and How They All Found Their Way Home*

Is there anything purer than a redemption story? Whether the redeemed is man or beast, you cannot help but root for the one who is desperately trying to find their way home. *Sanctuary* gives us not only a beautiful story, but a wee bit of permission to believe in miracles and the hope that those we love who are lost can be found once again.

KATHI LIPP, bestselling author of *The Husband Project* and *Ready for Anything*

sanctuary

The True Story of an Irish Village,
a Man Who Lost His Way,
and the Rescue Donkeys That
Led Him Home

sanctuary

PATRICK BARRETT
and SUSY FLORY

TYNDALE
MOMENTUM®

The Tyndale nonfiction imprint

Visit Tyndale online at tyndale.com.

Visit Tyndale Momentum online at tyndalemomentum.com.

TYNDALE, Tyndale's quill logo, *Tyndale Momentum*, and the Tyndale Momentum logo are registered trademarks of Tyndale House Ministries. Tyndale Momentum is a nonfiction imprint of Tyndale House Publishers, Carol Stream, Illinois.

Sanctuary: The True Story of an Irish Village, a Man Who Lost His Way, and the Rescue Donkeys That Led Him Home

Designed by Ron C. Kaufmann

Edited by Bonne Steffen

Published in association with the literary agency of The Steve Laube Agency.

For information about special discounts for bulk purchases, please contact Tyndale House Publishers at csresponse@tyndale.com, or call 1-855-277-9400.

Library of Congress Cataloging-in-Publication Data

A catalog record for this book is available from the Library of Congress.

ISBN 978-1-4964-4500-1 (HC)
ISBN 978-1-4964-4501-8 (SC)

Printed in the United States

28   27   26   25   24   23   22
7   6   5   4   3   2   1

I dedicate this book to my mother, the strongest, most caring person I know. I love you with all my heart.

And to my soulmate, Eileen. You are the brightest light in my life. You embody love. There is never a dull day with you in it. I love you.

CONTENTS

FOREWORD

You just never know where life will take you. One day I was working as a sales manager for a computer company, and the next my life had forever changed. My office was located on the seventy-eighth floor of Tower One of the World Trade Center. On September 11, 2001, I escaped the tower safely, along with my brave guide dog, Roselle, and within hours the media learned about my story. Nine years later I received a phone call from Susy Flory who was writing a book about dogs and their tales. After hearing what had happened to me, she said we should write a book together. And suddenly, overnight, my life took another turn. We collaborated and in 2012, *Thunder Dog* was published.

I have been around dogs all my life. I have been teaming with guide dogs since 1964. Some of the most remarkable experiences I have ever had have been forming a real team relationship with each of the remarkable guides I have had the honor to meet.

Patrick Barrett, whether he realized it at first or not, was also creating similar bonds with rescued donkeys. More than once, those relationships saved his life. In so many ways, this book shows the value of each creature God has created and why we should never take our animal friends for granted. As Patrick Barrett demonstrates, when we help—through love—each creature we meet, we also, sometimes in unexpected ways, help ourselves to be better.

Sanctuary is a love story on several levels. It is a memoir of a man who encountered many life challenges and overcame them. Right from the beginning, I was drawn in, and I just knew Patrick would come through and persevere even at his lowest point, all because of his donkey friends. I hope you find a quiet place and let yourself be drawn in by the word pictures Susy and Patrick paint.

I believe every book, fiction or nonfiction, teaches us something. Some books' lessons are more powerful than others, and the stories these books have to tell are made all the more poignant when written by great storytellers. Sit back and be prepared to go on a real-life journey with Patrick Barrett. Together, he and Susy Flory tell a great story.

Michael Hingson

RAISED BY DONKEYS

❖

Who do you think set the wild donkey free,
opened the corral gates and let him go?
I gave him the whole wilderness to roam in.

JOB 39:5, MSG

I GREW UP ON THE BACK OF A DONKEY, a restless daydreamer who loved setting out to explore what I would come to see as paradise, although I didn't really appreciate Ireland until I nearly lost it.

I live, and I belong, in an ancient village called Liscarroll in the province of Munster in the southernmost part of the Emerald Isle. We know which people live in what house, and the people before them, and the people before them. We cross ourselves when we pass by graveyards and we know who lives in those places too. We have thousands of years of history and it's in our bones and our blood, our stories and our songs. We're a land of dreamers, story keepers, and storytellers.

In the olden days, Munster was one of the kingdoms of Gaelic Ireland, ruled over by a king of kings, or *rí ruirech*. My namesake, St. Patrick, spent several years in our area, founding churches and training holy men and women to carry on the work he had started. Later, the Vikings and then the English arrived, with much blood spent on both sides in the cause of freedom. We Irish are known for fierce resistance against any and all oppression, and we are fighters, although we haven't always won. We're also lovers, and we love our ancient sports, our whiskey, our heritage, our villages, and our families.

Liscarroll was a magical place to grow up. There was a holy well called *Tobar Mhuire*, Gaelic for Mary's Well. People brought pieces of paper with their needs scratched in pencil and tied bits of cloth to the trees around the well. There is a ruined stone church, an ancient graveyard full of ancestors, and the great Liscarroll Castle, with four massive round towers looming over one end of the village.

As a boy I loved to run around inside the ruins, pretending I was a warrior fighting off the bad guys and saving the day. I remember a local lad running atop the stone wall one day and falling off. It was a long fall and he crushed his ankle, but that didn't stop me. I had battles to fight!

Among the rolling green fields around the village were strange groupings of trees, perfect circles of oak, ash, hazel, birch, and willow, called fairy rings. No farmer dared cut down these trees or in any way disturb these unearthly places for fear of what mischief the angry fairies might bring upon his head, so they've been untouched for centuries. While the crumbling castle didn't scare me, I had more respect for the fairies and left them alone. Ireland is a place full of stories, legends, and mysteries, but to me it's just home, so it is.

My early life was a bit like a fairy tale. We lived on a beautiful farm in the green hills of County Cork, crisscrossed by mossy stone boundary walls wrapped in brambles. That family farm became a donkey sanctuary where thousands of donkeys were rescued because Mam and Dad had soft hearts and open arms for all living things. When my dad saw a donkey that needed help, he brought it home to my mam.

My mam's name is Eileen and everyone says there wouldn't be a donkey sanctuary without her, and that she helped my dad's dreams of helping the donkeys come true. But back then she was just Mam, a typical Irish mother, strong and no-nonsense and the backbone of our little corner of Ireland, showing her love in the kitchen. I felt her love every time she fed me and my three older sisters, Debbie, Helen, and Eileen, with scones hot from the oven.

The donkey sanctuary was on our family farm, but my mother *was* the sanctuary.

Mam and Dad started the sanctuary because the sad truth is that we Irish have not always loved our donkeys as we should have. For hundreds of years, these funny four-legged creatures have served our people willingly and well. People loved the work they did—carting fresh milk to the creamery; transporting seaweed from the beach; bringing vegetables to market, haystacks from the fields, peat from the bogs; and bearing people on their backs or pulling them along in carts. Many is the donkey who found its own way home with his owner asleep in the cart, bumping along behind after a few too many pints at the pub.

Yet the donkeys didn't have much work to do once the tractor invaded Ireland. As a result of mechanized farming, there were thousands of donkeys all over Ireland who were no longer needed, and sometimes people got too old to take care of them or gave up on them when they became sick and left them by the side of the road to die.

But some of the lucky ones were truly seen and, like my first and best long-eared friend, Aran, picked up and rescued. I learned just about everything I know from Aran and the other donkeys who were part of my life—Timmy, Jerusalem, Penelope and

Peanut, Guinness, Tinsel, Nollaig, and Jacksie. Each one showed me something different about myself and how to live.

Now that I'm older, I've realized I'm a lot like a donkey because I don't always want to do what I'm told. It's not easy to bend a donkey to your will, which is why they sometimes end up abused. They have their own minds and opinions on things and sometimes choose not to obey.

Donkeys are much more than humble beasts of burden; they're smarter than horses, strong-willed, and very, very intuitive. If they're lucky and well cared for, they can live for fifty or even sixty years. They are also strong, resilient, loyal, and very hardworking. They live in big herds and stay together, taking care of each other like big Irish families.

But even though I had my own herd—a human family that was always there for me, with parents who did their best to raise me right—there was a time when I got separated from my family and the donkeys and lost my way.

I was born into an Irish fairy tale, but the fairy tale fractured.

At the sanctuary, I grew up in the donkeys' shadow, but I know I wouldn't be here today if it weren't for these stubborn and beautiful creatures. I grew up in a kind of Eden, but when I got older I left my little corner of paradise. Yet the sanctuary had my heart, and my soul was tied to the rock at the top of the hill behind our house, my favorite place in the world. Even in my darkest days I carried a picture of the village and the castle and the rolling green hills of Liscarroll in my pocket.

The donkeys have always been there for me, loving me, accepting me, and believing in me when everyone else had all but given up. I learned how to talk to them and, even more important, how to listen to them. The donkeys led me home, back to the crumbled stone watchtower at the top of the hill where the donkeys gather.

And one night, when all seemed lost, God met me right there at the rock.

My life has been a series of tests. With some I have chosen well and passed, and with others I have not. But I am blessed because my mam and dad started a donkey sanctuary to save lost donkeys, never dreaming it would save me, too.

CHAPTER ONE

ÒRE∂(ƆIΠG
UIT℧ J∂CKSIE

⊕

*Fairy tales are more than true: not because they tell us that dragons
exist, but because they tell us that dragons can be beaten.*

NEIL GAIMAN

JACKSIE IS A FUZZY BROWN, SILVER, AND WHITE Irish donkey with
a creaky voice and a big crooked grin. His mother didn't want
him, so he has lived with my family from his very first days, and
he has always thought he was human. When Jacksie first arrived,
tiny and starving, he needed a big bottle of milk every three hours
around the clock.

Whenever it was my turn for the night shift, I'd build up fresh
straw around us into a cozy nest and wait for Jacksie to start nudg-
ing his tiny velvety white nose against my hand.

"Are ye hungry now? Hold on, Jacksie. It's coming."

I reach out and rub his withers, showing him the bottle and
shaking it gently. Jacksie tilts his head, the tangle of fluffy hair at
the top almost hiding his shiny black eyes. His ears are almost as
big as his head, downy white inside and tipped with dark brown

at the top, like they've been dipped in chocolate. His muzzle is pure white, his lips pale pink, and below is a tangle of soft curly baby whiskers.

As soon as I point the bottle toward him, he lays his ears back along his head and lunges forward, grabbing the nipple and gulping the warm milk as he gazes into my eyes. I feel a twinge deep inside. I always do with Jacksie.

He's adopted me as his brother and during the day, whenever he hears my voice on the other side of the fence, he starts squeaking and honking in his baby voice—he can't bray yet and won't for a while. When I first open the gate, he tries to wrap his neck around me in his version of a hug or nibbles on my arm with his gums. He just wants to be part of my herd.

About halfway into the bottle we settle in and start to hear the other donkeys on the grounds of the donkey sanctuary, hundreds of them going about their nightly rituals in the barns. Some stand in the straw all night long, alternately munching on bits of hay and grain before lapsing into brief standing naps. Some lie down and sleep soundly, legs twitching a bit, dreaming of galloping through luminous green pastures on sunshine days. Others are more restless, moving around inside the barn, listening and watching, standing guard and giving out a bray when they hear a fox cry out in the fields. Jacksie's ears lift up a bit and twitch as he listens to the herds. Someday he will join them.

As Jacksie's tummy begins to fill and his gulping slows, his soft gray eyelids begin to dip down. His eyes are lined in black, flared at each end like an Egyptian makeup artist painted him with kohl. Around the black is a narrow line of white fur and thin silvery eyelashes.

The heat lamp overhead casts a rosy glow and I pull off my jacket, then let myself sink down and lean back into the warm straw. Jacksie goes down to his knees and starts to burrow, his back tucking into my right side. His nose pops up again, and I crook my arm up and around his head, holding the bottle at just the right angle so he can drain the last few drops.

My eyes are getting heavy too and as I look at the bottle, I catch the shine of the scar, a jagged half circle, slightly raised, snaking across the underside of my right forearm. Then I fall asleep with Jacksie, and as the bottle drops from my hand into the straw above his head, my dreams about the dark-haired boy start. I know the young lad is me, but it feels like I'm watching a film and I haven't been a lad for a long time.

I'm standing on top of a big rock at the crown of a green hill and I can feel the wind blowing my hair. The rock points to the sky, and the flat surface on top is my favorite place in the whole wide world. My grandmother, who lives in the stone house below, says the rock is left over from a stone watchtower that crumpled a long time ago. Now I'm on watch, and I look down on the lane that runs through the middle of the village.

I can see the great ruined castle at one end—a big gray rectangle with a massive tower at each corner, built with limestone from the old stone quarry on my grandmother's farm. I conjure up bands of Irish warriors in dark green tunics and leather boots, holding oak shields in one hand and gleaming swords in the other, fighting off the bad guys and saving the people of the village. Someday I want to be brave and strong like that.

But for now, my brave steed isn't a great war horse—not even close. He's a small barrel-shaped donkey with gray and white patches, fuzzy ears, and stubby legs. His name is Aran. He lived with a very old man who couldn't take care of him anymore, and that's how he ended up on our family farm.

In my dream Aran trots up to the rock and I jump down, give him a hug around his neck, then vault onto his back. "Let's go, Aran!" He runs for a bit, then slows down to grab a bit of grass. I lean down and rest on his neck, my arms around him. He's the first donkey I ever made friends with, and when I feel alone, he comes to me. When I feel scared, he comforts me. When I feel invisible, Aran sees me. We are family.

I slide off and we walk down the hill together. It's getting dark, and Mam will be worried about us. We walk side by side, Aran and me, and when we get down to the gate, Mam is there, ready to whisk Aran into the barn and then me into the house for dinner. Everyone says Mam has a way with donkeys. She can speak their language and get them to do anything she wants.

Outside my dream a donkey brays in one of the barns, and Jacksie stirs next to me, rustling around in the straw and wriggling a little closer. His back makes a warm spot against my side and his breathing slows again as he falls back asleep.

This time I stay awake but go into some kind of a dream state—half awake and half asleep—and this dream is a darker one.

I'm in a city, all concrete and paved roads and cars roaring by. The air is stale and sour, no breeze or smell of grass. People pass by me but don't look my way; I feel invisible. I keep walking, and everything looks the same. I'm hemmed in by dingy old buildings and nothing ever changes.

I stop and look at my reflection in a big window.

Who are you?

The carefree lad from the rock is gone. Instead, a man with flat black eyes looks back.

What is wrong with you?! Why is everything so messed up?

I shake my head and run my hand over my face, then look again as the pain begins to build inside.

Why can't you get your life straight?

I want to shout and cry, but I know that if I start, I'll never stop. I barely recognize the face in the window anymore. I've lost who I once was and become a man infused with darkness and wreathed in shadows.

I can't stand to look at him anymore, so I make a fist with my right hand, draw it back, then put all my strength behind it and punch my hand straight through the massive window, breaking the glass and shattering the reflection of the man with the shadow eyes.

Then baby Jacksie stirs again, rolling over and rubbing his forehead against my arm. I reach down and stroke his neck and ears. I'm fully awake now, ready to get back to the house and crawl into my own bed.

I pull a bit of straw over his long gangly legs and leave him snoring peacefully in his warm nest, dreaming of scampering around green pastures with the herd. Then I'm off to rejoin my own.

CHAPTER TWO

ARAN THE ESCAPE ARTIST

❖

A good friend is like a four-leaf clover,
hard to find and lucky to have.

IRISH PROVERB

I DIDN'T KNOW I WAS GOING TO MEET my first and best friend when I rode along with Dad to pick up Aran. I was seven years old, and not only did I love going to work with my dad, but bumping along the roads of Ireland in our green Jeep towing a Rolls-Royce trailer that had been donated to the sanctuary was an adventure all in itself.

The roads of Ireland are lined with ancient stone walls covered in vines and flowers—daisies, wild roses, foxgloves, and bluebells—with green fields full of sunny yellow bunches of ragwort stretching out beyond. In some places, thick forests grow up along the walls and meet overhead, causing your car to go dark as it shoots into leafy tunnels. In other places bright moss, and sometimes even thick grass, grows right on the surface of the road and you're rolling along over a brilliant ribbon of green.

Everyone drives fast, dodging massive rumbling tractors with big wheels, lorries belching smoke, and hedge trimmers clipping the overgrowth with long arms. People walk the roads with their kids and dogs, and sometimes you need to squeeze by horses and riders, bicycles, or sheep. You have to slow down in the villages and watch out for older people and more dogs, and on top of that the signs aren't always good (and are often in old Irish, what some call Gaelic).

But that doesn't matter, because when you grow up in Ireland you have the roads in your head. You know who runs which shop or pub, because they and their families have been there for hundreds of years (and you're related to some of them). You know the old stone barns, cottages, and the ruined towers, monasteries, and castles. They're all just part of the landscape, like the trees.

People have lived in Ireland for many thousands of years and have left parts of themselves and their stories behind, but that was my normal. So was tagging along on Dad's rescue missions to save the donkeys. That was one of my favorite things to do—much better than sitting in school listening to my teachers drone on while I looked out the window and dreamed of being out in the fields with the donkeys.

After a quick ferry ride across choppy water—it was my first time on a ferry, and I was a little disappointed Dad wouldn't let me out of the Jeep—I saw a lonely donkey. He lived in a field all by himself out on Inishmore, one of the rugged Aran Islands in the Atlantic Ocean off the west coast of Ireland at the mouth of Galway Bay. Inishmore is the largest of the Aran Islands and is known for ancient sites like the prehistoric clifftop fort called Dún Aonghasa and the Worm Hole, a rectangular natural pool in the rock. The islands were full of sacred places—stone crosses and altars, ruined churches and monasteries. In one field is a well called

St Ciaráin's Well, where tradition says a huge salmon appeared to miraculously feed 150 monks.

The island was populated with several hundred people, mostly living on farms marked off by stone walls patchworked in lichens and moss. When we drove up and the aged farmer showed us his donkey out in the field, I could see his raw, red skin peeking out between the patches of gray and white hair on his round body. He looked like he hurt, and I winced like I felt his pain inside my own body. We walked over, and I shuddered at the big open sore on his withers.

"Oh, I don't know where that donkey came from," said the farmer. "He wandered into our plot here." The man was older, frail looking, in farm clothes and Wellingtons with a thin wrinkled face under his cap.

Dad looked at me, and I instantly understood—this man *was* the owner but just wanted to get rid of the donkey and didn't want to accept any of the blame for his condition. Dad knew what to do: Avoid a fight and get the donkey out of there as fast as we could before the farmer changed his mind. The donkey's safety and welfare came first, so we needed to get him into the trailer and back to the sanctuary.

While Dad talked to the man, I explored the fields, looking for a castle or a fort, but found only stones. When I came back, Dad was looking the donkey over.

"What is wrong with him, Dad?" I wanted to reach out and touch the poor donkey and somehow take care of his sores, but I didn't want to hurt him more. Not only was his skin a mess, but he was skinny, his ribs and hip bones sticking out.

"Aye, this one's got the rain and wind scald," Dad whispered.

My dad's name was Paddy, a common nickname for Patrick. I was named after him and I wanted to be just like him; he was so good with people and seemed to be able to handle just about any situation. I looked up at Dad's round face with his fair skin and kind green eyes under a wool cap. I could hear the pain in his voice.

"We need to get him inside and get him warm, where he can heal up," he said.

Rain scald is a common donkey ailment. The harsh environment of cold sea winds and rain had kept Aran wet and, after many years, had eaten away his coat. Donkeys originate from hot and dry parts of the world, so their coats and skin don't do well with cold, rainy weather like ours. They need shelter. To live, this donkey needed a safe, dry place so he could recover. I was happy we could give him that place.

"Can we call him Aran?"

Dad smiled, then nodded.

"Hi, Aran," I said, trying out the name. We were about the same height, and once I could see past his skin condition, I began to look into his dark eyes, ringed by silky silver hair. Something about him and his eyes ignited my imagination.

What are you like? I wondered. *What are you about?*

When Aran looked back at me, I felt something I'd never felt before—a little tickle in my heart like a small electric charge. We were curious about each other, but we were both a little scared.

Then, in a rush, I felt like I was with Aran in a much deeper way. Through his big ears I could hear the crashing of the waves onto the rocky beaches of the island, and in his torn skin I could feel all the cold and the wet and the loneliness and the misery of his life and his days. It was a flash of understanding, as if I could see the world through his eyes. I saw into him, and I could feel what it was like to be him.

Aran had been all alone, forgotten by the people who were supposed to care for him. He had been starting to forget what it was like to be with people, donkeys, or any living creature other than the sea birds soaring high overhead. Aran had no herd.

I felt sad, because I knew donkeys cared about each other.

I couldn't wait to get to know Aran better. I longed to see what this little scruffy ghost was all about. There was a connection between the two of us, and the tickle in my heart was slowly turning into a pure feeling of sheer joy.

The farmer seemed relieved to let him go, and even though Aran was skittish at first because he wasn't used to being handled, Dad worked his magic and got him into a halter. Dad always carried carrots or Polo mints or a small bit of ginger with him—donkeys love the smell of ginger. I hopped up into the trailer and pulled on the lead rope while Dad gave him a push from behind, and Aran walked right up inside. It was like he knew there was a better place for him somewhere up the road.

Aran was quiet on the way home, even as we pulled the Jeep and trailer on the ferry and chugged back across the water to the mainland. I wondered if he'd miss the sound of the sea or the taste of the salt on the thin grass. I hoped he'd find some friends at the farm.

We had about sixty donkeys at the time, separated and sorted into fenced-off sections of the fields. Because donkeys love to eat everything all the time, we had to keep them from eating too much rich, sweet grass and getting sick.

Dad fastened loose plastic collars around their necks, red for the boys and yellow for the girls, with their names written in black marker so we could easily tell who was who. Some already came with names and some, like Aran, didn't. While he was named for the islands he came from, the name Aran originally comes from *Aaron*, a Bible name meaning "mountain of strength." But my Aran was more of a disheveled little hill than a mighty mountain.

I watched while Dad made a collar for Aran and put him in the barn to let him rest from the journey. Mam came out to doctor him with some medicated creams and sprays for his skin and feet. While she worked on Aran, I heard her talking to him quietly.

SANCTUARY

"Come on, boy, you're okay," she said. "*Tch, tch.* Come here. Head up there." She continued grooming him, checking him over, giving him scratches behind the ears and hugs around the neck.

I couldn't hear everything she said but it was a soft, melodic murmur, almost like she was singing him a song. It made me smile. I think I saw Aran smile too. I bet he loved having a sweet-smelling, beautiful mam taking care of him!

Within an hour Mam had Aran thoroughly convinced he was in a safe place with a new herd and a matriarch who would take good care of him. The neglected, anxious donkey who had arrived in such poor physical condition now felt loved and protected.

While Mam worked, I ran to grab a carrot from the feed room. When Mam was done, she said, "I think he's ready for a treat." Her lips formed a slight smile and she patted me on the shoulder before she went back into the house to make dinner. That big show of emotion from Mam made me happy. I knew she loved caring for the donkeys almost more than anything else in the world.

I waved the carrot in front of Aran's nose, thinking he'd reach out and grab it with his lips the way donkeys do, but instead he turned around and ignored me. You know it's happened when you're staring at their hindquarters and long skinny tail like a big, upside-down paintbrush in the middle.

"Aran, don't you want a carrot?" I waved it again, tempted to poke him in the leg with it, but I knew that might get me kicked. Donkey kicks were to be avoided at all costs.

Wait—maybe you've not had a carrot before!

I let my hand drop, still holding the carrot, and waited. And waited. I probably waited five minutes—which is a very long moment in boy-time—until I gave up, turned around, and decided to run back to the house. And that's when it happened. Before I could take even one step, I heard a small noise behind me. I stopped still.

12

Mam always moved slowly around new donkeys and gave them some space. "Let them get used to looking at you, and to your smell," she said.

So, copying Mam, I turned my back to Aran and pretended I was frozen, like a giant ice cube, with my hands by my side. It was really hard to stand that still. Then I felt it—tickly whiskers on my wrist, and his fuzzy lips nibbling at my fingers curled around the carrot.

Slowly, oh so slowly, I turned around partway and rotated my hand at the wrist to hold the carrot out toward him. This time, it worked! His lips reached out like fingers and grabbed the carrot, pulling it away from me and munching away. Aran just needed some time. He didn't want pressure; he wanted to do it his own way. I watched his face and I think when he was finished chewing up the carrot, he gave me a small smile, just like Mam.

In the days ahead I found the more I turned my back on Aran, the more he wanted to get close. If I tried to put a halter on him or grab his collar and walk him, he stopped. If I pulled hard he'd turn into stone, his back end starting to go down until he was almost sitting. I didn't know he knew the ice cube game! Except Aran was stronger than me, and he could be an ice cube as long as he wanted. I couldn't force him to move; I had to wait him out.

It wasn't that Aran didn't know what I wanted him to do—he just didn't want to do it. He wasn't used to being walked around by a human, and while he was a little scared, he also had his own ideas about where he wanted to go and what he wanted to do. But the more I gave him time and space to decide on his own, the more comfortable he became, and the more he started to follow me around like a friendly puppy.

For the first three or four weeks, Aran stayed in a wooden box stall of his own at the top of the yard with fresh, sweet-smelling straw to sleep in and a split door so he could peek out. This cozy new home helped him get used to the sights and sounds and smells of the sanctuary, a much busier place than his lonely outpost on Inishmore. It also gave Mam a chance to watch him and see if he had any health problems or anything contagious that she didn't notice at first. While Aran was in temporary isolation, I visited his stall every day before and after school, talking to him from the door.

"How are ye today, Aran?"

He came forward, his eyes bright and his lips twitching in hopes of another fat carrot.

He decided very quickly that he liked me coming by, and he always looked me in the eye and gave me that funny feeling inside. Even when I wasn't with him, I felt that tickle in my heart every time I thought about him. *Aran likes me!*

As our friendship grew and Aran got healthy again, with shiny new hair now covering his damaged skin, I started spending more time with him in the fields. I loved watching his every move and how his big fuzzy ears twitched back and forth separately, like television antennas. I started trying out different donkey sounds to see what he responded to. He seemed to like some more than others, and I kept trying to find the right pitch.

My family thought it was funny, and I enjoyed their laughs and teasing, but I was serious and worked hard to mimic the sounds. I'd never known any other human who could bray exactly like a donkey, but I had plenty of furry teachers to help me hone my new skill. I genuinely wanted to communicate with the donkeys in their own language.

After a while I started hiding and trying out my donkey calls, sneaking around in the dark, peeking around a corner, or hiding in the tack room and watching the donkeys through a hole in the wall to see if I could trick them into thinking I was really a donkey by singing my best donkey song. I loved when it worked and they kicked off, a bunch of them braying in unison like some mad donkey choir.

I also liked to lie down in the grass next to where Aran was grazing and watch his face from ground level so I could see what he saw. I spent hours every day looking at the curly silver whiskers on his soft muzzle, a top lip that could twitch all around and nuzzle my hand, or twist and snatch a piece of apple from my fingers. Every time, I felt that feeling again—like he could see all the way into me, and he liked what he saw.

Aran cared about me and kept an eye on me. I noticed how sensitive he was to his environment and how he signaled his feelings through the movement of his ears, which swiveled back and forth or went flat back against his head. I learned to watch his nose, feet, and tail, which all reflected his mood. I knew he watched me too, and when the weather allowed, I was out in the fields with him for most of the day. There was such a lovely feeling about him.

I started riding Aran bareback around the farm and up the hill to the rock. I mastered the art of jumping up onto his back and steadying myself with my left hand on his neck, while giving him a soft smack on the rump with my right hand. My dad couldn't ride him because most donkeys in Ireland are too small for an adult. But they are the perfect size for a kid, and my sisters Debbie, Helen, Eileen, and I would ride—especially Helen. She was my sister with red hair like Dad, and she, too, seemed to have a special way with the donkeys like Mam.

I rode Aran all over the fields with just a rope halter or a bit of twine looped over the top of his head, around his jaw, and over his nose, with a bit of length left over for me to hold on to. His backbone stuck up, forming a sharp ridge, but I learned how to sit comfortably behind the dark gray cross on his neck and shoulders. I guided him with a slight shift in my body weight to send him forward, slow him down, or turn him to the left or right. He responded to my cues—when he felt like listening to me, that is.

Whenever I rode Aran and touched the cross on his back, I remembered the Jesus story, which I heard something like this:

A poor farmer near Jerusalem owned a young donkey. One day two men came by, saw the donkey tied to a tree, and asked the farmer if they could have him.

"That animal can't carry much," the farmer said.

"Jesus of Nazareth needs it," one of the men said.

The farmer handed them the rope, and when Jesus first saw the donkey, he bent his head down, smiled, and stroked his neck. Then he climbed on the young donkey and rode away to the city of Jerusalem, where the crowds waited with palm branches and welcomed him with shouts of joy.

The donkey loved his gentle master, served him well, and later followed him to Calvary. The day Jesus died, the shadow of the wooden cross where Jesus died fell upon the shoulders and back of the donkey, leaving a permanent mark. To this day, many donkeys bear the imprint of a cross on their backs.[1]

I loved this story, and I loved riding an animal Jesus had ridden. I felt like my family and I were special because we were the family in Ireland called to care for this sacred animal that carried Jesus. It was so long ago, but I often wondered what that donkey must have felt, and I liked to think about how he had been faithful in carrying out his service. It made me love Aran all the more, because one of his kind had carried the Son of God on his back.

After a few months of good food, grooming, and care from Mam, as well as a safe place to stay warm and sleep, Aran's memories of his cold and lonely life on the island began to fade away. The other

---

[1] Adapted from *The Donkey Companion* by Sue Weaver (North Adams, MA: Storey Publishing, 2008), 11.

donkeys gave him room to just be, and he slowly started to find his place in the herd.

"He's coming around," Mam said. The joy in her voice gave me that same feeling in my heart.

Then something surprising happened—Aran decided to join our family herd too! Even though he was making friends with the other donkeys, I had spoiled him with carrots and the occasional slice of bread and he followed me everywhere, hoping for more treats and back rubs. One day he showed up at the back door, pushed it open, and clip-clopped right into the house.

"Aran!" said Mam in the kitchen. "What are ye doing in here? Get out!"

Aran didn't seem to know *what* he was doing in our house, but I could tell he was happy to be there. He turned out to be an escape artist and learned how to unlatch two gates to get into our backyard, then nudge open the back door of our house. Donkeys are good with their lips—they can stretch them out in all directions and use them like fingers. He let himself in whenever he wanted to join us while we were eating dinner or watching TV. I sometimes sneaked leftovers to him—a bun or scone or toast. He was like a Hoover with hooves.

Once Aran learned how to get into the house, he'd walk right past the kitchen, sneak into the hallway, and peer through the door to the sitting room. He was stealthy and could get all the way into the sitting room without making any noise at all. Suddenly you'd see his fuzzy face peeking around the corner. I imagined him tiptoeing through the kitchen and it made me laugh every time I thought of it. And he never once went to the bathroom in the house.

My parents used to laugh at him until he got a little too comfortable in the kitchen, and Mam was afraid he'd get hurt with something hot on the stove. But when she tried to turn him around in the kitchen and steer him back outside, it was quite the operation. It's not easy maneuvering a barrel-shaped donkey in a small space.

Aran never got to stay inside for long, but I thought he was brilliant. Every single second I was with him was a good one. We were on the same frequency, and I never felt lost when he was around.

CHAPTER THREE

MAM'S LEG

✠

*A single sunbeam is enough to drive
away many shadows.*

ST. FRANCIS OF ASSISI

MY FIRST DAY AT SCHOOL I gripped Mam's leg with all my strength
and didn't want to ever let go. I was so scared I couldn't look up,
only stare at her brown shoes with cream-colored soles. The hills
of Liscarroll were my playground and the donkeys my teachers.
So it was a very rude awakening when I realized I was going to
have to leave the sanctuary where I felt safe and go spend my days
inside an old building, reciting dull facts, and doing sums and
memorizing poems in the Irish language that my tongue seemed
to always tangle up.

I lived in my daydreams, and I always had a film playing in
my head that was much more interesting than what went on in
school, where I felt lost and disoriented. I must have always had

a distant look on my face, because a typical interaction with my teachers went like this:

> Teacher: "Where are you, Patrick? What's going on with ye?"
>
> Me: My stomach tightens because I've already learned that Irish teachers can be very strict. I don't answer. I fidget.
>
> Teacher: Frowns. Shakes his or her head. Goes back to the lesson.
>
> Me: I let out my breath, relieved. And the film reel starts up again in my head.

This happened over and over not because I was being difficult or disrespectful, but because I didn't know how to express the places I went in my head, where my imagination reigned.

The real answer I couldn't say was, *I am looking down from above.* I could go deep inside myself, into some kind of inner workings, and it was almost like an aerial view looking down at the lad sitting at my wooden desk, wishing he was outside looking for adventure in the lost worlds of warriors, battles, and castles. The schoolroom could not contain me.

In my mind's eye, I could see scenes from the past, the battles and the bravery around the castle and the watchtower. I'd picture Aran out in the fields with his new herd, exploring the farm and grazing around the rock. Sometimes I'd dream about the future, where I'd be a soldier fighting for my country, or maybe playing Gaelic football or the ancient Irish game of hurling. I wanted to make my village proud, but I had a feeling it wasn't going to be through my schoolwork.

One subject I did like at school was history, where I learned the complicated story of our land—from the ancient Irish to the Celts, the Vikings, and the English, and the wars and battles we fought. I also loved the story of St. Patrick. Patrick was my great-grandfather's name, my father's name, and now mine. Being named for a famous saint made me feel special, although after I went to school and struggled to fit in, I realized special doesn't always mean good. Sometimes it means you are the odd one out.

St. Patrick was kidnapped in either Wales or Scotland as a teenager and carried to Ireland on a slave trading ship. When he arrived, he was sold to a local chieftain who used him to tend sheep and pigs. Alone and hungry in the freezing cold, Patrick started praying and getting to know God. Much later, after a miraculous escape from Ireland and a vivid dream that drew him back, he made friends with the Irish, learned the ancient language, and traveled around the country sharing Christ with the people. He spent several years in our part of Ireland, founding churches and training holy men and women to carry on the work he had started. The Irish embraced Christianity and Patrick became a legend for his faith, courage, wisdom, and kindness. I was proud to have his name and know his story.

Local history was important to all of us in the village. Liscarroll was considered a rebel stronghold in Cork County, which called itself "the rebel county," and some of the local families lost their sons and brothers in the War of Independence in the early 1900s. Our village legend, Paddy O'Brien, fought back against the English, and I grew up hearing the stories of his fierce courage, strength, and leadership.

Liscarroll is a typical Irish village. One narrow main street is lined with one- and two-story stone houses fitted closely together, with brightly painted red, blue, and green doors, lace curtains in the windows, and whitewashed walls. At one end of the village looms the castle with its massive stone towers, and across from the castle is an ancient ruined church and cemetery. The graves of our ancestors are marked by stone Celtic crosses covered with lichen, many of them tilting and sinking back down into the earth. At the other end of the street is the school and The Old Walls pub. Liscarroll Church, built of dark gray stone, stands at the center. Green rolling hills dotted with sheep, cattle, and donkeys surround the village, which looks like a small island of silvery stone in a sea of wild green waves.

On summer days, with Mam and Dad busy with the donkeys, my grandmother was often the one taking me into the village along with my sister Eileen. As we set out from her big rock house next door, we'd go left, walking along the road with a big green hill on the left and a wide grassy valley on the right with a stream running down the center. We followed the road as it curved around to the left, and within minutes we could see the cottages and shops of Liscarroll off in the distance, with the castle standing guard over the village and the green fields rolled out like a carpet all around.

As we walked toward the village, we could smell typical farm smells—manure piles, fresh cut hay, and silage burning. My ears picked up pigeons cooing in the trees, ravens squawking and swooping overhead, tractors rumbling, kids playing games on the pitch, church bells ringing at nine, twelve, and six o'clock, and the occasional wild cuckoo call off in the distance. Always, no matter where you were in the village, there was a background chorus of donkeys up on the hills having a chat—complaining, disputing, excited about feeding time, shouting a warning, or maybe just celebrating the day.

Sometimes Eileen and I would run toward the village, barking and acting like dogs, probably driving my grandmother crazy and embarrassing her in front of her friends. Along with my donkey call, I also practiced mimicking dog, cat, and other farmyard animal noises, and I learned to throw my voice so you couldn't tell where the sound was coming from.

Once past the castle, Main Street was busy with people talking over the latest village news and going into shops and pubs. Weekends were the busiest. My favorite place was the sweet shop run by an old lady. Her shelves were lined with big glass jars full of beautiful homemade sweets and my favorite were the clove rocks, red in the middle and white on the outside. My grandmother would buy me a bag of clove rocks for 50p and I would savor them for ages.

-+◇———◎ ◎———◇+-

Liscarroll Castle, built of local gray limestone back in the 1200s, is one of the largest Norman castles in Ireland. At one time there was a moat in front, with a drawbridge leading up to a massive stone tower house protected by a big iron gate that slid down from above. This gateway area is vaulted inside with several rooms on top, including a banquet hall and bed chambers.

Through the gateway is a massive open rectangular courtyard, which at one time had wooden buildings inside for people and animals. Across on the other side is a smaller gate tower plus four big circular towers, one at each corner. The English attacked us here back in 1642, and legend says there is a hidden well and a secret escape tunnel called "Hole of the Green" that comes out on the other side of the hill. But I never found it, though I looked.

There were arrow slits, murder holes, and spiral stone staircases inside the towers. There was a portcullis, and an opening in the gate tower roof where you could climb up and out. When you were on top, it felt like you could see to the ends of the earth.

In my daydreams, Aran was my loyal steed—short and chunky legged though he was—carrying me away to freedom and adventure. I wish I could have taken him with me everywhere, but alas I could not. On school days I had to leave Aran behind, put on my itchy uniform, wash my face, comb my hair, and go sit at a desk.

Mam would get me up at about 7:45 in the morning after she'd already been outside to mind the donkeys. The cats, Marmalade and Socks, and Spot the dog, all slept at the foot of my bed, keeping my feet lovely and warm and making it hard to get up. But when Mam's voice got more serious, I'd jump out of bed, stand by the radiator, and put on my school uniform—gray pants, white shirt with maroon stripes buttoned all the way to the top, and a long-sleeved wool jumper in the same maroon color as the stripes on the shirt. I pulled on my socks and laced up my black shoes, then went into the bathroom to wash my hands and face and comb my hair. I fed and watered Spot, then ate my porridge of Irish oats laced with a spoonful of sugar and some hot milk. Next came a cup of hot tea and toast with marmalade while Mam made lunches for Eileen and me.

Mam was very regimented in her lunch making and packed my trusty Bovril sandwich on white bread and a pint of creamy milk in a glass jar wrapped with a tea towel. Bovril is beef paste, a horrible tarry liquid stuff with a tangy taste that stains your teeth. It smells rank, and most people make a hot drink out of it, not a sandwich. My mam grew up eating it with her brothers and sisters. The kids at school used to think it was chocolate spread and would steal my sandwich, taste it, and then get sick, which made me laugh. It is disgusting, but I loved it and still do!

If the weather was good and it wasn't raining, I'd walk out the back door and be greeted by Spot, Socks, and Marmalade, now gathered around the coal shed behind our back lawn. Just to the right of the shed was the big gate, which opened out onto the fields where the donkeys roamed. I always brought a few crusts of bread, and Aran and Spot would join me to walk toward my grandmother's house next door.

Halfway to her house was a big forty-foot-high linden tree—in Ireland we call it a lime—which I used to climb to get my blood pumping. Spot gave up on me at this point and headed back home. After jumping out of the tree, I'd finish the walk to my grandmother's house and open the back door to the smell of tripe cooking for her beloved Alsatian guard dogs, Rex, Rudi, and Heather. My grandmother would have a mug of Ovaltine with milk for me, and I'd down it and spend a few minutes with the dogs. Then I'd head out back to her hen shed to see how many eggs had been laid.

I passed by the gray and white barns scattered around the foot of the hill and then the old limestone quarry, which looked like a small dry pond dug into the hill on my right where the cats liked to hang out. Beyond the quarry were the pastures, some on the hills to my left, some on the right, and some up ahead bordering a stream where the foxes and badgers had holes. At the stream I turned right and climbed up the steep hill and through the trees. On the right stood a majestic old oak tree with a swing.

Next was the wicket, an old rusty gate by the oak tree. Once I was through the gate I jogged past a line of bushes and came out on the top of the hill where the landscape opened up, the sky bigger and the world of people a little smaller. It always gave me a sense of freedom to follow the donkey pathways meandering toward the rock. The smell of the fresh meadow grasses and the movement of the branches in the wind on the ash, lime, and oak trees conjured up in me a sense of belonging.

As I ran through the fields and up and down the hills with my school bag bumping across my back, Aran would trot alongside me on the left, like an escort. He matched my stride, whether I walked, jogged, or ran. It's like we were joined together. I wasn't talking to him; we were communicating on some other level. If

I was sad or upset, he'd be with me and seemed to understand what I was feeling, as if he were soaking in my energy. I would feel his, too, which was calm and peaceful and steady. It felt like we were in unison with each other and it grounded me, like a buffer against my fear and anxiety about school.

Being at the top of the hill with the rock and the old ruined fort was like being at the top of the world. I could turn around and look out in all directions, the wind blowing and carrying the sounds and smells of my world. I was surrounded by farms and animals, grass and trees and flowers—and donkeys, of course. I felt free and peaceful up there.

On the rock I could also look straight down into the hurling pitch. I loved hurling, which is like a combination of baseball and field hockey, sometimes savage, always exciting. Just like every other local lad, I started training before the age of ten and dreamed of being a great hurler on the school and club teams and making my village proud.

After a good look around, I jumped down off the rock where Aran was waiting, and before I ran down the hill, I reached over and gave him one last scratch on his withers. I'd run off and he'd trot back to the herd. It was always a lovely moment that sent me down the hill with a little smile on my face and joy in my heart. I'd jump over Dan Canty's stone wall, run across the hurling pitch and head into the village, where I could smell the peat smoke curling up from the cottage chimneys.

"How are ye, young Barrett?" was the typical greeting from people who saw me, and I'd nod or lift my cap.

When I passed the church, I'd make sure to bless myself before I arrived at school. St. Joseph's was the village school next to the church, and there was a lot of pressure; I felt as if the saints were frowning down from above, like when I stood on the rock and looked down on the village and the castle. After I got to school and joined the line of kids outside the front door, the first order of business was morning prayers together as the church bells rang at nine o'clock.

We sat in chairs at wooden desks, two to a desk. I always seemed to be paired with Roy Gardner, the only Protestant kid I knew and a great friend to play warriors with, using branches for swords and tree bark for shields. Roy always presented well compared to me. I was more rough-and-ready with holes in my trousers, dirt on my shoes, and the smell of donkeys on my hands. I took baths, but only every second or third day when Mam forced me.

Teachers in Ireland can be tough on kids—sometimes too tough. If I wasn't in school, I was constantly on the move, and today I'd probably be diagnosed with dyslexia and attention deficit disorder. But back then I think my teachers thought I wasn't paying attention or trying hard enough. Liscarroll is in a part of the country where many people speak the Old Irish, and while I knew a few words, my parents didn't speak it and I wasn't fluent. Memorizing long poems in Irish was part of the schoolwork, and if I forgot a line or mispronounced a word, I knew a beating was going to come. I saw or heard words differently than other kids and schoolwork felt hard, like it was frying my brain.

I almost always felt like I didn't belong or was invisible, and I wanted to get back into the fields with the donkeys as soon as possible. It's a terrible thing to feel unseen and unheard, and that's when I started to get into trouble.

By now I could meow like Marmalade, bark like Spot, and bray exactly like Aran—even the donkeys themselves could no longer tell my voice apart from one of their friends. I'd been working on my donkey call for a long time. I practiced and practiced, fueled by some kind of inner energy that I couldn't always control. I knew there was going to come a day when others would recognize this special talent, and I wanted to be ready for it. I even could throw my voice, making it sound like a meow or woof or bray was coming from around a corner or outside a window. The teachers were beside themselves, not knowing where the animal noises were coming from.

Donkeys have quite the vocabulary, unique among members of the equine clan, because sound comes from both sucking air in (the *hee*) and breathing it out in a mighty rush (the *haw*). Donkeys love to neigh and bray and don't wait for an excuse to fill their lungs with air and sing their hearts out, usually stopping only when they get short of breath.

By studying my buddy Aran and his friends, I learned to imitate different calls, such as "Get out of bed and come feed us. We're starving!" or "Where is my friend? She was here just a second ago!" or "It's morning, I'm happy, and I feel like making some noise!"

I also noticed donkey songs vary in pitch and volume not only between male and female donkeys (also known as jacks and jennies), but between different sizes of donkeys. Miniature donkeys squeak, while mammoth donkeys have the lungs and voice of an Italian opera singer. Some donkey voices are creaky like a set of uilleann pipes, some are joyful and clear as a brass horn, and some have the power of an old tractor engine, cranking up to a high and rhythmic crescendo loud enough to make your heart stop.

If donkeys don't want to break into full-throated song, they might decide to utter a string of conversational grunts and groans, like a rusty metal door on squeaky hinges, or a series of melodic hums. I loved all of their noises and kept practicing my donkey calls all the time.

Pretty soon I was good enough to fool the donkeys and thoroughly annoy my parents, especially my sisters. I drove everyone mad and learned I could start the donkeys braying in the shed early in the morning and listen to the rollicking chorus spread across the fields and into the village, waking everyone up. I was waiting for just the right moment to try it out in the schoolroom.

At first I tried hard to behave in school, with the saints and Jesus watching. Growing up Catholic in Ireland means growing up with lots of eyes on you—eyes of those alive and dead and in the heavens above, at all times of the day and night.

About the time we got Aran, Mam read me a story in the *Illustrated Children's Bible* that haunted me. Although we prayed the Rosary every night before bed, Mam didn't seem that religious. But she did read the Bible to me and Eileen. I was fascinated by the pictures of the Holy Land, with beautiful palm trees and donkeys in colorful harnesses with tassels among the golden sands of the desert.

One night I had a dream about walking through the Holy Land on a long journey through the desert. There were palm trees, just like the pictures in the Bible, and a donkey walked beside me. It felt like the two of us were headed somewhere and carrying an important message.

Another night Mam read the story of Jesus being tempted in the wilderness, and the story and pictures of Jesus facing off against the devil penetrated my heart and my spirit and wouldn't let go. I was terrified, yet fell asleep only to experience the terror all over again in a vivid nightmare. I can still remember that feeling. After that I had nightmares every night about the devil and I knew he was real. I wanted to be a good Catholic lad, follow the rules, and stay away from the snares of the devil. A feeling of intense dread hung over me much of the time and I prayed at night in bed, my hands together, but I felt like God was an angry old man in the sky who was ready to punish me for breaking his rules.

When it came time for my first Holy Communion, Mam dressed me up in a new black suit, white shirt, and red tie, and while she tied my tie I rehearsed in my head everything I'd learned in the catechism. Since I wasn't the best reader, I listened carefully and became good at memorization.

During the service the priest gave a message, and whenever he'd ask a rhetorical question, I'd put my hand up to answer, piping up in a loud voice. I wanted to make sure the priest and the blessed Lord knew I had all the answers. The whole congregation was laughing at me but I didn't care. I wanted to get it right.

While I had the answers, I also had a powerful fear around God. I didn't carry his love with me; instead, I carried a heaviness from the temptation story along with the feeling of being tested, found wanting, and perpetually unable to keep God happy. It was a heavy burden, but I wanted to be good for him and for my mam and dad, who worked so hard to take care of all of us and to help the donkeys.

But the fear of God and the love of my family and of Aran weren't enough to keep me from danger. When I was seven years old, about a month before my first Communion, my grandmother offered me a glass of sherry, and my life was never the same.

CHAPTER FOUR

TIMMY & TEA
WITH TRAVELLERS

⊕

*The Irish are the heaviest tea drinkers per capita in the world,
averaging four to six cups per day with many people drinking even more.*

ANNA SNYDER, IN "IRISH TEA CULTURE"

A NEWBORN DONKEY FOAL named Timmy came into our lives a few
years after Aran. Timmy was dark brown and very fluffy, with a
huge poof of messy hair right over his eyes. He had a big, energetic,
cheeky personality and was easy to love. But his mother, Greta,
didn't want him. Even though she had carried him for a full twelve
months, from the moment he was born she lashed out at him.

No one really knows why a mother donkey rejects her baby like
this. Maybe Greta was in terrible pain from the birth process; labor
can be quick, or it can take a whole day. You can see the pain in a
jenny's face as she stands there with her ears back, head down, and
mouth open. She might appear calm, but donkeys are stoic and
you know she's in pain.

Or maybe as a new mother she was confused by what had just
happened and who this little stranger was. Greta was young; she

had come into the sanctuary already pregnant and still bonded to her own mother, so maybe she wasn't ready or willing yet to be a mother herself. We knew there was a problem when she didn't act like she knew him, or seem to really notice him. She didn't lick him or nicker to him or act protective either.

Dad and Mam kept a close eye on Greta, holding her tight and using gentle words and nudges to encourage her to take care of Timmy and let him nurse, but the situation got worse and she began to pin her ears back and bare her teeth at him. He was just a defenseless little guy who wanted to be loved and fed and kept warm, and instead he was being treated like he was the enemy.

When Greta began to try to bite and kick him, it was time to intervene. A donkey's kick can be very dangerous, especially to a newborn, and with Timmy's life in grave danger, Dad and Mam and my sister Helen managed to pull him away from Greta and bring him over to the house to try to save him. They put him in our garage (which doubled as a barn for the babies in need), and we all helped take care of him. At the time Helen was dating a guy from the village named Tim, and that's where little Timmy got his name.

We took turns bottle-feeding him and Mam taught me how.

"Look, this is what ye do now," she said, sprinkling some warm milk from the old glass bottle onto her finger.

"Make sure you hold it firm and let him get a taste of the milk." Timmy sniffed her finger and began to nuzzle at the drops of milk.

"Now don't leave it to dribble down his neck," she said, tilting the glass bottle up and down to control the flow as he latched on to the big rubber nipple. Timmy caught on quickly and started gulping down his breakfast.

As I learned to hold the bottle for Timmy, Helen teased me because I'd only weaned from my own baby bottle at five years old.

I'd loved that soothing feeling of warm milk in my stomach and hadn't wanted to give it up. I still have good memories of sitting on the sofa between Dad and Mam, leaning on her shoulder, cozy and enjoying my bottle. It gave me a lovely feeling of everything being right in the world. I got called a baby, but it was worth it. I finally weaned off my bottle after a trip to the seaside, where Mam told me she left the bottle behind and couldn't get it back.

Even with a rough start, Timmy took to the bottle in Mam's capable hands and we took turns bottle-feeding him every three hours. He bonded closely with all of us, and before long he was following Helen or me into the house whenever he could. He was smaller and cuter than Aran, so he got away with even more mischief. He began nipping and biting and trying to play boisterous donkey games that were fine for donkeys but painful for humans. He'd surprise me, dashing out from a corner and nipping at my elbow, leaving a nice little mark. I had to wheel around and cup my hand under his chin to keep him from biting me. Helen was the only one who could do anything with him.

I couldn't understand why Timmy's mom had acted that way, but maybe there was something wrong with her that we couldn't see. It seemed so unfair, and it didn't make sense to hurt someone you were supposed to take care of. How did his mam not see him for who he was? My heart hurt for him. But Timmy's problem with his mam was something like what was happening to me in school.

The first few years of school had not been terrible. Although they'd had to pry me off Mam's leg and I would rather have been at home running around the farm, I did start to look forward to the stories about Ireland, especially the warriors and battles. I had a favorite teacher in fourth class named Gerald Lenihan who loved hurling and Irish football and told us great stories about the castles and battles of Ireland. I really looked up to him; he was very strong but fair. He never raised his voice, but we all listened to him. If you stepped out of line, he put you in your place in a kind but firm way.

I loved the stories about Fionn Mac Cumhaill (*mc-cool*), a powerful Irish warrior in the northern tip of Ireland who threw giant boulders during a battle with another warrior. Mac Cumhaill's rock throwing created the Giant's Causeway, a massive rock bridge you can still see.

I also loved stories about the Red Branch Knights and their most famous hero, Cuchulain (*coo-coo-lunn*), which meant "hound of Cullan." Cuchulain was a mighty warrior, handsome and well loved by all, who served the king. He was said to have seven toes on each foot, seven fingers on each hand, and seven pupils in each eye. He also had magical weapons, including his sword, his visor, and a barbed spear that he used to win many epic battles. Supposedly his battle cry could kill a hundred warriors from fright alone, and when he went into battle he transformed into a crazy figure with wild hair, a bulging eye, feet that faced backward, and blood spurting up from his head. His body grew so hot he could melt snow, and when he fought in this state, he was uncontrollable.

As a boy on the verge of adolescence, these heroic tales ignited my imagination. At home I was surrounded by mostly women, with my mam and three sisters in the house and my dad busy working in the sanctuary. I wasn't sure what it meant to be a man yet, and so these tales of warriors and their epic deeds were acted out again and again with my friends using stick swords and bark shields.

My cousin Gary was a year older than I was and the closest thing I had to a brother. His dad was my uncle Brendan, my Dad's brother, who was killed in a farming accident when I was young. Gary used to visit often from his home in nearby Killavullen, and we'd scramble up to a thicket of bushes, blackberry brambles, and oak, blackthorn, and hawthorn trees close to the top of the hill.

We called it a "cover," and we'd get down on our hands and knees and climb through the tunnels inside, made by foxes, badgers, and hares. It was like a maze inside the cover and we'd get lost, scramble to find each other, then get lost again. During school I'd daydream about exploring the green tunnels, and I could smell the primroses and bluebells even when I was at my desk. My favorite time of day to be in the cover was at dusk, when it got a little eerie.

One day Gary and I were running around up by the cover and saw a strange sight—a person with flowing red hair in a long robe, like the Celtic attire we'd seen in books and movies. At first, the red hair made me think it was my sister Helen dressed up in a strange costume for some reason. But then the figure turned and I saw it was a man. He looked at us, and then in the gathering dusk he faded away into a silhouette. Gary and I got spooked and ran back down the hill to the house. We sat at the table and laughed ourselves silly, but we never found out who the man with the long red hair was or what he was doing there, though I wondered if he somehow came out of the old crumbled stone tower.

Another good friend was Brendan O'Connor from the village, whose two aunts owned a village pub called Fitzgibbon's. I used to ride my red BMX bike down to the village to meet him and we'd ride around together, play Irish football, or practice hurling. The village was our playground, with the castle towering over it. When we rode past the pubs, I watched the delivery trucks rolling the big barrels of Guinness in through the doors. I could smell the scent of beer wafting out and see the men overflowing onto the footpaths on the weekends, laughing and joking. Maybe that was what being a man meant! I couldn't wait to be part of that scene, and I loved it when I was with Dad on a donkey rescue call and he'd take me with him to the pubs for a Coke so he could have a drink when the work was done.

In fifth class the schoolwork got harder—especially the reading—and that's when the beatings began. The headmaster of the village school was an older man nearing retirement, with the nickname Jazz. He was burned out and always seemed angry. The class picked up on this, and it caused a rebellious atmosphere in the classroom. Some of the kids called him "the tyrant," and my sisters had warned me about him. Eileen said he was very cross.

It was a vicious cycle—Jazz couldn't keep order in the class and struck out daily in frustration. With my challenges at school I was the weakest link, and whenever I couldn't get a sum right, mispronounced an Irish word, or decided to try out my donkey call, I'd suffer the consequences . . . and they were always physical. My frustration and shame at my inability to do the work drove me to mischief, and I started playing the clown. I was embarrassed and felt awkward, and so I became someone I really wasn't. I didn't want anyone to know or see the real me. My sister Eileen, however, was a brain box. School came easy to her, and I didn't see why it had to be so hard for me. Why couldn't I be like Eileen?

I might have seemed a little mischievous, but inside I felt like the kid who nursed on a bottle until I was five and hung out with the donkeys. I felt embarrassed to have a dad who wasn't a farmer like the other dads, but someone who ran a donkey sanctuary (the only one in Ireland) and drove a big green truck with the sanctuary's logo on the side. I didn't want to stand out; I just wanted to be like the other guys and fit in, not be the laughingstock of the village. I grew resentful, feeling like the donkeys were more important to my parents than I was. It was a lie I told myself, but I began to feel I was raised in the shadows of the donkeys. To hide all this anger, I learned how to play the chameleon and act like I thought a man should act, and that involved becoming something of an ass. Ironic, right?

Jazz saw what was going on with me, and he didn't like it. In the end I think he decided to make an example of me since I wasn't doing the work and was trying to make light of it so the other kids would laugh. When the tyrant got angry, he'd march over and grab me by the ear or grab a handful of hair on the side of my head and yank me out of my seat, drag me across the classroom, and throw me into the corner, then slap me on the cheek or the chin. It stung and left a smack rash. I didn't tell my parents, but I'm sure they saw my face and heard what was going on. Being beaten was not only painful, but it was confusing and humiliating. I wasn't the only one; other kids were beaten too, and it all happened in full view of the class.

The first few beatings I suffered in silence. Feeling like a complete and utter messer, I figured I'd earned it and I could take it like a man. This kind of thing was normal for a lot of Irish teachers, and Dad had been beaten as a boy too. But the continuing harsh treatment finally got to me. After three or four beatings, I couldn't take it anymore. We didn't even treat the donkeys this way. In fact, when someone beat their donkey like this and it was reported, the donkey was taken away and ended up with us, courtesy of the humane society.

The last time it happened, I was in trouble for mispronouncing a particular word in an Irish poem and Jazz dragged me out of my seat like he always did. This time he beat me for about twenty minutes in front of all the other kids—who were frozen in their seats—until I fell to the ground.

Is this ever going to end? I thought, curled up in a ball.

I cried with the pain, and then I cried with anger and embarrassment. I felt like a complete failure. *Everyone in the village must know what a mess I am.*

I couldn't take it anymore so I got up on my knees, wrenched myself to my feet, and in a surge of rage like Cuchulain, I raised my hands and shoved him back as hard as I could. He tripped over a school bag on the floor and fell backwards. I froze, looking down at the hated headmaster now lying on his back, defenseless.

Out of the corner of my eye I saw a few of my schoolmates' faces. Some were in shock, and some were even crying. I was still bawling like a lost calf.

A thought struck me. *He's going to beat me even more.*

Then a worse thought. *He might even kill me.*

I knew this was what Timmy must have felt like, when the person who is supposed to care about you and take care of you actually hates you. It was different than when Mam hit me with the wooden spoon. That didn't really hurt all that much, and I knew I deserved it and that she loved me and would still bake me scones. This was different. It felt like Jazz despised me.

I panicked, adrenaline racing through my veins, and started breathing hard in anger and then in fear. *If he gets up, he could kill me!*

But as my flash of rage began to melt away, I was faced with the reality that I'd just knocked down the headmaster and I was going to be in big trouble. My family was going to hear about it, the village was going to hear about it, and I was going to be looked down on as a failure and a disgrace to my family.

I didn't know what else to do, so I turned around and ran away, across the classroom, out the door, and down the road toward my house, rubbing my eyes and trying to squeeze them shut to hold back the tears. I ran away from my class, my friends, and that school, and I never wanted to go back. It was going to be hard for me to trust teachers again after that, when I already felt I didn't belong and wouldn't ever be able to do the work like the other kids.

I ran all the way down the road to my grandmother's house and burst into the front yard where she was working in the garden. She always wore a pretty skirt and cardigan with a high-necked blouse and her hair done up. I, however, was a mess. I was still crying and in some kind of shock, with bright red finger marks and scratches on my cheeks and neck.

"What's going on?" she asked, eyes wide. "What's happened?" It was lunchtime, and I shouldn't have been there until school was out at three. I don't remember much after that. She took me inside, and the rest is a blur. I remember telling her I didn't want to ever go back. She seemed pretty angry, especially when she saw my reddened skin.

I'm not fully sure, but I think she drove down to the school the next day to talk to them about it, and Jazz was forced to retire soon after.

My grandmother wasn't scared of anything, much less a head-master. She was a typical Irish grandmother—strong and not much for hugs and I love yous—but always ready to feed you something and fill your mug or glass.

Her big two-story rock house next door to ours was built with beautiful cut stones taken from a mysterious ruin nearby called Ballybeg Monastery. Dad said the Vikings had ransacked it and then burned it, and I heard a kid say there might be treasure buried underneath. We all thought the stone house was haunted; maybe the monks had put a curse on anyone who stole from Ballybeg. But Grandmother certainly wasn't one bit scared of Jazz or any ghosts!

I tried to forget what happened at school, to bury it deep inside and never think about it again. After the beating I became tougher, growing an armor and wrestling hard with friends. I took up mar-tial arts and started play fighting, and my gentleness with Aran and Timmy melted away as I tried to act more like Cuchulain than St. Francis.

But I did feel sorry for the donkeys who came in with scars or injuries. It happened all the time—if a donkey refused to do something, or did it too slowly, they were beaten. I knew the donkeys felt the same way I had when they were rejected or attacked. It was soul-crushing. Even though I was trying to get tough and act like a man, I still had that connection with the donkeys, especially the abused and hurting ones.

So whenever I could, I went with Dad on his journeys around the island to collect the donkeys and bring them back to the farm. We'd be gone several days at a time (and sometimes I'd get to miss school for a day or two), meeting the kind of people I never saw in our small village.

I loved watching my father deal with tough customers, some of whom weren't at all sure they wanted to give up their donkey, even if it was in bad shape. He treated everyone he met as an equal, no matter their background, situation, or origin, and he talked to them with respect. His wisdom shone through in some very tricky situations, because sick or injured donkeys don't always show the extent of their pain or illness.

When someone reported a sick donkey, the owner would often deny that there was a problem, and then Dad had to determine if the donkey was really ill and needed our help, and how he was going to convince the owner to surrender the donkey to us. As poorly as some people treated their donkeys, they also seemed strongly attached to them, and this made Dad's job harder.

A donkey can often be in pain and near death before anyone notices something is wrong, and it typically comes when a donkey lies down and refuses to get up. Sometimes their hooves get so long they grow outwards and start to curl up, crippling the donkey's legs. Sometimes the farrier can fix their feet with slow and careful trimmings over time. Sometimes the damage is too severe and the animal has to be put down.

Donkeys are tough and resilient and put up a strong show on

the outside. It took me a while to understand how this worked, but after the headmaster's beating, I could really relate. Sometimes survival means building up a strong wall around your true self, but it can be very hard to take the wall down once the danger is past.

Dad's philosophy was that in any abusive or neglectful situation, the donkey needed help, and his job was to defuse the situation so he could get the donkey out. He wasn't a judge or a jury (although, if needed, he could see to it that legal charges were brought against those who deserved it); instead, he was there to get the donkey to safety. Thus, kindness and a sense of humor were important.

Also, a cup of tea.

Tea is appropriate for just about every occasion in Ireland, and especially when a talk needs to happen. Dad and I drank tea in some unusual places, including cups brewed over small gas stoves in wagon caravans with the Travellers. The Travellers are a distinct ethnic group, sometimes nomadic, who have their own culture and traditions. They are a close-knit community, and they only marry or hang out with their own kind. They're proud and feel like they're the first real men of Ireland, with a history that goes back to the original inhabitants of the island. They have their own language we knew as *Cant* but also speak English with a thick accent.

Travellers are also known for their physical strength and for bare-knuckle boxing. Raising and trading horses and donkeys (they say "dun-keys") are a big part of their culture, and they are often present at horse fairs. Even if one of their donkeys is ailing, they treasure it so much they hate to give it up. Thus the many, many cups of tea Dad shared with them as he built bridges of friendship with this proud group of people.

Tea isn't the only important drink in Ireland. We're always drinking something. Whether it's creamy milk from the Kanturk

Creamery, a hot cup of tea brewed from a Barry's tea bag, a drink of spring water from a tin cup at a holy well, or a glass of lukewarm, coffee-colored Guinness, you won't go long without being offered something to drink. It's good Irish manners to politely refuse the first time tea is offered to you, again on the second, and then to accept on the third. It's the Irish way to sit and talk over a mug or a glass. It's how we connect. Maybe it has something to do with the cold, rainy weather or the centuries of oppression and violence, but we're looking for comfort and we connect over what we're drinking.

The Irish also have a reputation for drinking a lot of alcohol. Babies were given whiskey mixed in their bottles or rubbed on their gums for teething. People drank Guinness to build up the iron in their blood. Mothers and grandmothers mixed up hot toddies on cold nights. It was normal to drink, with family-owned pubs in every town serving as the center of community news and camaraderie around a cozy peat fire on cold rainy nights.

That's why, back when I was just seven years old, it wasn't all that unusual for my grandmother to offer me and my sister Eileen each a small crystal glass full of sherry.

"Here you go," she said with a smile.

I didn't think twice. I laughed and took the glass, gave it a quick look, smelled the beautiful pale golden liquid, and then drank it. She offered me a second, and I drank that too.

The sherry trickled down my throat and into my gut, and immediately a feeling of warmth spread down my arms and legs to my feet and hands. When the tiny flame of warmth made its way up to my head, I was in heaven, feeling lightheaded, excited, and very, very happy. I didn't ever remember feeling like that before.

I was much more used to feeling anxious, shy, lost, awkward, and wracked with worries and guilt. It wasn't just the dyslexia or being the only boy in a family of girls or having a dad who started a donkey sanctuary. There was something more. As a kid I could pick up other people's feelings, just like I had been able to do with Aran the first time I met him and could feel something of his memories and experiences like they were my own.

This happened with people too. I could sometimes feel the feelings of people around me, and it felt like they were my own, even though they weren't. It was my normal and I didn't know any different; I thought everyone soaked in other people's feelings like that. I didn't understand what was happening or what to do about it, and carrying other's people's emotions was heavy and hard. I wasn't even sure what my own feelings were yet, and here I was dealing with other people's too.

But those two little glasses of sherry did something magical, numbing all of those feelings that I didn't know what to do with. My first taste of alcohol seemed to immediately launch me into a much more carefree place, and I could tell my sister felt the same way. It reminded me of the story of Peter Pan and how he carried the children away to a mystical never-never land where everyone was happy and carefree. That's what the sherry felt like to me. I liked it.

When we got back home, I step-danced around the kitchen, grabbing Mam and getting her to do a few steps with me. I made everyone laugh. I went to bed with my head spinning and my heart full and happy from the loads of attention. I thought it was brilliant, the best day I could ever remember, and I woke up the next day still feeling happy.

A few days later I was back at my grandmother's house, and all of a sudden I remembered the sherry. It was like the bottle was calling to me from the cupboard. I waited until she was busy, then I tiptoed into the kitchen, opened the door of the cupboard, found the bottle, and took a sip. Then another. I closed my eyes and felt the warmth and the joy again.

I was at Grandmother's almost every afternoon, and after plenty of stolen sips of sherry, there came a day when my grandmother noticed the bottle was almost empty. I'd been caught! I wasn't sure what would happen, but she started laughing at me. She gave a little shake of her head. "No harm!"

I didn't know what to say and turned tail and ran out the door, but she thought little Paddy stealing sherry was about the funniest thing she'd ever seen.

That was the end of it for her, but not for me. Aran wasn't the brightest spot in my life anymore. I'd made a new friend—the drink.

As I got older, and life got a little tougher, I quickly started to rely on alcohol to get me through. When school was hard, I could look forward to a drink with my friends, some of whom had access to alcohol from family-owned pubs. After the beating happened, I drank whenever the painful memories bubbled up. When I felt guilty or ashamed of myself, I washed away the feelings with alcohol.

My friendship with Aran had been an anchor for me, but now I'd found something better—something that made me feel more comfortable in my own skin, less awkward, and less of a loner. *I am on my way to becoming a true man.*

CHAPTER FIVE

A Kiss
of Faith

✤

I can resist everything except temptation.

OSCAR WILDE

THERE WAS A GIRL in the village named Eileen. There were many Eileens in my life—my mother, my sister, my grandmother, and an aunt. But there was only one Eileen Healy.

Eileen grew up in the village just down the street from the sanctuary, and she was in the class below me. She had shiny dark hair, laughing eyes, and fair skin that glowed like a sunrise. I thought her beautiful.

I heard a story about an orphan lamb the Healy family was raising. It slept in the kitchen in a warm spot under the front of the stove and took to following Eileen out of the house and down the street to school. Even the creatures could see she was smart and beautiful with a big, warm heart.

Eileen and I would see each other around the village every once in a while, but she didn't seem to notice me much. Once she got mad at me for a prank I pulled—maybe it was when I climbed up a tree and threw water balloons down at the runners in the club she was part of—and she wrote in her journal, *I hate Patrick Barrett.* She showed it to me with a small smile. At that moment, I knew I loved her, with all the love an adolescent can muster.

Once when we were teenagers, we had a moment, Eileen and me. There was a pub called The Old Walls at the opposite end of the village from the castle. They had beautiful homemade food—all of my favorites, including fresh-baked brown bread, bacon and cabbage, roast beef, wild mushrooms, and mouthwatering puddings.

Every Thursday night, The Old Walls had a dance and everyone in the village turned out for it. Plenty of matchmaking went on between the set dances, and clusters of kids stood around speculating about which lad fancied which girl, and vice versa, and what they might be going to do about it (which was usually nothing).

When I arrived with my friend Barry, I saw Eileen there with her friends and I immediately felt more nervous than usual. She looked pretty, her eyes friendly, and I fancied her but I just wanted to run away. I was too embarrassed to ask her out or even talk to her, afraid she might laugh at me.

But my friends and her friends orchestrated us being together outside at the exact same time. Somehow the stars aligned and it happened. Our lips met. It all happened quickly, but it was my first kiss and it felt like a miracle.

Barry and I left soon after and I was walking on air, but sadly, the relationship really didn't go anywhere. After that magical evening, Eileen and I exchanged a word here or there around the village. My heart always beat a little harder when I saw her, but the great romance was over before it ever really began, and deep inside, I was afraid that she still hated me.

Maybe I didn't deserve her, because the sweet naive lad I used to be was starting to go a bit wild. Instead of getting up in the morning and walking through the fields with Aran or Timmy, I stayed in bed as long as I could before I got up and threw on my uniform—gray pants, gray shirt, and a blue tie. I wasn't at the village school anymore—after I ran out the door on the day of the beating, my parents sent me to a school in Kilbrin, a nearby town, and Mam used to drive me there in the car and drop me off. No more walking through the fields up to the rock every morning. I missed my touchstone.

I didn't care so much about the Bovril sandwiches anymore, but I had to have my cigarettes, a habit I picked up. First thing in the morning I was smoking John Player Blues with some other boys in the park. I wasn't too interested in school, either. Getting up to mischief is what I looked forward to, and I had that—as well as the cigarettes and drink—in common with my new friends. I had joined up with a different herd.

My new school, called *Schoil Mhuire* (Mary's School), was a religious school at a convent run by the Sisters of Mercy. Believe it or not, I loved my religion class best. Our teacher, Sister Teresa, looked the part in a navy-blue skirt, sweater, and hood. She seemed ancient but she was actually an adventurous woman of the world who had been a missionary in Africa; she had plenty of stories about famine, disease, and the drug lords she'd met. I don't remember the lessons as much as I remember Sister Teresa's adventures.

She told a story about one village woman whose stomach was swollen. The woman thought she was pregnant, but her stomach got bigger and bigger, accompanied by excruciating pain. Finally she died, and inside her body was a giant tapeworm the size of a snake. With stories like that, Sister Teresa always had my attention, and I listened to every word she said. She seemed full of wisdom and had me looking at the world in a different way. I wanted to get out and see some of the world like she had.

My world had also expanded a bit through sports. I was in the fields with the donkeys less, and more often down at the pitch on the other side of the hill with my hurling stick. Paddy O'Callaghan, an old man who loved the sport, was often down at the field and he offered to help me. Sports were my escape from thinking about myself and my worries, and I spent hours practicing with Paddy and another village lad named John Buckley. I was fast and wiry from running around the fields of the sanctuary with the donkeys, plus cleaning their stalls and pitching hay. But the level of competition between John and me was unbelievable, and we played obsessively.

Hurling is one of the oldest field sports in the world and looks like hockey with a baseball, but it's much more intense. An observer once said, "Hurling is war by other means," and you often come away from a match with blood flowing from one body part or another.

Here's how it works: You run around a big grassy field (what we call a *pitch*) with a curved wooden stick, called a *hurl* or a *hurley*, made from a single piece of ash wood. The large flat end at the bottom is almost like a blade, and you sprint around the field with your team, trying to lift or strike the ball with your stick or hand. You can also kick the ball up and through the goalpost, which looks like a y-shaped American football goalpost. Hurling is considered to be the fastest ball game in the world, and it takes skill. You need to keep your eye on the ball at all times and accuracy is key. In some matches, a player may score from 60 to 70 metres away from the goalpost.

When you get good, you can run at full speed with the ball balanced on the hurl, before flipping it high into the air and whacking it over or under the crossbar of the goalpost. We didn't use helmets or pads at the time, so there were always injuries due to the hard ball, the tackling, and the sticks flailing around at high speed. When I was a teenager, the matches were much more gory and bloody than they are now, and I loved it.

Competitive team sports have always been important to the village, a crucial part of our identity. I worked my way up through the ranks and age groups with my friends Sean Murphy, John Buckley, Brian Brosnan, and Brendan O'Connor. The Gaelic Athletic Association oversees everything, but it is more like tribal warfare than anything else, village against village, with Cuchulain's hurling myths fueling the ancient fires. The matches are social events and a place to see your friends or catch up on what's going on with the local families. If you're a good hurler in the village, you're looked up to. I practiced hard and became pretty good, enjoying the attention. I would hate to have been a young lad without hurling because I wouldn't have known what to do with myself.

It goes without saying that you have to either have courage or be slightly insane as you dive into the fray headfirst toward the ball, ash wood chips from sticks flying everywhere, with no time to think and no room to pull back out. I adopted the motto of one of our trainers: "Be ruthless within the rules." My parents didn't attend the matches, and that may be the reason why. Think of taking a wooden axe to the neck or the head, and you'll have a good start on understanding the sport.

During the season I was constantly beat up, bruised, and bleeding onto my jersey, but the more you got beat up, the more you learned to protect yourself. The girls played with us early on but phased out into their own teams as we boys got bigger and stronger.

I'd finally found a place where my high energy and scattered attention became an asset. I became the main go-to man for scoring goals and points and was treated to many a drink in the pubs afterward, even though I wasn't of drinking age yet. Between these congratulatory drinks and a friend whose family owned a pub and could get us various forms of alcohol, I no longer needed to sneak drinks from family cupboards. I found plenty on my own.

But even with all the camaraderie of hurling, I still never felt part of the team. A deep sense of isolation and alienation plagued me. I didn't have a strong sense of belonging anywhere. I had worked my way into plenty of herds—not just with the donkeys, but with my own family and friends from various schools and teams I played on, but something was missing. I yearned for that deep feeling of connection I had early on with Aran and the other donkeys, and the sense of peace and safety I had at the top of the rock. That feeling had melted away, and I always felt like the odd one out.

The euphoria from playing sports never lasted long, and I had a nagging feeling that I was a big disappointment to my parents, due to my failures at school. My marks would never make them proud. They also wouldn't have been proud of my smoking and drinking, so I hid that from them as long as I could.

But I didn't waste too much time feeling guilty about anything either. This was my new normal. By the age of fifteen or sixteen, I was hanging out—smoking cigarettes and drinking beer—with the boys and making them laugh with my donkey calls. On the weekends, Brendan O'Connor and I did odd jobs for his aunts at Fitzgibbon's. When I could, I'd sneak into the pub's storehouse and come away with a few bottles to share with friends.

On school days, I'd come home and maybe see Aran for a bit or maybe not—I always knew he'd be there, and I sometimes caught a view of him standing and waiting for me—and then into the house to eat and watch TV. I began to forget him with my mind on other things, like my next cigarette. The house was busy with my sisters and other family and friends coming and going, so we usually didn't sit and have a meal together. We did still say the Rosary before bed because Mam made us, but saying prayers was more of an obligation than anything else. My early interest in God had receded into the background and so had my vivid fears of his anger and disapproval. I just didn't think about God much. I was starting to get more interested in sports, girls, and always the drink—that's what it meant to be a man in my book.

Weekends I stayed in bed as long as I could and then left the house as quick as I could to get away. My parents were busy with the donkey sanctuary, so they had a hard time keeping track of me, and I didn't make it easy for them. I'd join the boys for hurling, then we'd climb up on the community center roof, accessed from the roof of a nearby garage and then a jump across a five-foot gap, to drink and smoke. No one ever caught us because you couldn't see us from the road.

We took to pranking, like the infamous water balloon stunt that made Eileen Healy so angry. I did break a window once and got in trouble for it. Another time, a member of our group fired up a motorbike belonging to Oliver O'Dee, a brilliant storyteller and daydreamer like me, and tore up the hurling pitch. The local *garda* showed up, confiscated the motorbike, and locked it up in the station. We got the idea to steal it back, but we never could quite work out how to do it.

For a time, we took to harassing a neighbor who lived across from the pitch. He had two big Alsatian dogs, and he must have heard us hanging around because he kept threatening to set the dogs on us. We threw rocks onto his roof, and one day he sent his dogs after us, but we jumped up onto the community center roof before they could get to us.

At fourteen, I'd been drinking for a full seven years and it had changed me. When I'd drink, first there was a buzz—a feeling that I was outside of myself, almost like a different person. I'd get comfortable, like I was starting to fit in with the group. I liked that feeling of being accepted. Then I got bolder and the normal intense feelings and emotions coursing around a young boy's body started to channel into new and angry feelings, all of which stirred up in me when I had alcohol in my system. I wasn't the cute lad anymore, high on grandmother's sherry, step-dancing around the family kitchen and getting laughs. But I was okay with the change and became convinced that drinking was a way out of my own head and worries. It never crossed my mind that there might be another, better way, and I worked up to downing two six-packs during a drinking session.

My sister Helen's boyfriend, Timmy, saw what was happening and tried to point me toward a different path. He was a brilliant hurler, strong and fast, a man's man. I looked up to him. He was also very honest, kind, and friendly, like a gentle giant. He let me play hurling with him and his friends, and with me being the youngest out there, he kept a good eye on me.

One day after a practice match, he sat down with me while we packed up our gear and looked me in the eye. My heart skipped a beat because I knew he was going to say something important.

"Paddy, mind yourself," was all he said.

I looked back at Timmy and then quickly looked down, feeling awkward. *What does he mean? Don't all men drink?*

While my feelings and thoughts and worries and fears were my constant companions, I wasn't one to feel guilt or shame. So while I registered his words and still remember them, I didn't apply them to anything I was doing. I never paused and stopped to contemplate my actions or think, *This might not be good for me.* I just went in the direction of the herd. Soon I began to be looked up to, a ringleader of mischief and drinking sessions. I heard whispers of what some of the parents were saying.

Don't you be with Patrick Barrett.
He's bad news.
Paddy will get you into trouble.
Stay away from him.

I was hanging with rougher and rougher kids, trying to feel like I was part of something bigger than myself. I couldn't wait to be eighteen years old and legal so I could walk into a pub on my own and order a drink. Then I'd feel like I really belonged.

When I was sixteen, a family secret came to light that added to my angry, confused feelings. My sister Eileen, the next closest to me in age, went to the cinema with our older sister, Helen. They were hoping for a lovely day together, but Eileen was consumed with sadness and had been for a while, though she didn't know why.

But Helen knew something Eileen didn't. "I think it is time you know the truth," she said when they got back home.

Eileen sat in her bedroom, heart beating hard, while Helen went to fetch Mam and Dad. Mam came in first, looking anything but her usual strong and kind self. Instead she looked vulnerable and afraid. She began to unveil the long-held family secret—Mam was not actually her birth mother. Instead, Eileen was my aunt's daughter, who bore her out of wedlock.

Dad came in at some point and sat on the bed with my sister and Mam, explaining that when Eileen was born, the plan was for her to be put up for adoption. But when my parents heard the news, they couldn't bear the idea and took her in to raise her as one of their own children.

When Eileen was about five years old, her biological mother and Mam had both wanted to tell her the truth, but our grandmother was absolutely dead set against it. Eileen believed she was our blood sister, as did I, and the years went on with the truth buried deep. It wasn't an easy secret to dig up and bring out into the open.

Secret family adoption was a huge risk in a rural Irish village of the 1970s. My aunt had been an unmarried twenty-four-year-old, and the typical Irish way was to send a pregnant girl away to have the baby somewhere else and be adopted out. Only then would the girl return to her family, all in deepest secrecy. At that time, single moms were looked down upon and couldn't receive Communion at church.

It was shocking for all of us, and most of all for Eileen, who had always felt disconnected. Helen and Debbie had known the truth for a few years but were sworn to secrecy—not an easy truth to keep to themselves all those years.

I was shaken by the news. Of course, it made perfect sense that my parents, who took in homeless donkeys, would take in a tiny baby who wasn't their own but was still their flesh and blood, and who desperately needed a loving home and family. But as a teenager wrapped up in myself and my problems, I felt like I'd been lied to my entire life. Suddenly I was finding out my sister wasn't who I thought she was. I felt deceived and confused.

I loved Eileen—we were so close. We'd grown up together playing in the fields with the donkeys, swinging beneath the old oak tree up by the rock, watching television, and eating our porridge together. We used to kill each other and love each other at the same time, sharing a room with bunk beds. Now I was just confused. *Is Eileen still my sister?*

I never spared a thought for what it must have been like for Eileen to hear the news. Where once I picked up on all of the emotions of the people around me, I'd now learned to block them out with my own desires and plans, most of which revolved around where to get my next drink. I was losing my connection to everything that kept me tethered—my sisters, my parents, and even some of my friends who tried to warn me.

Helen and Timmy got married, and he asked me to be a

groomsman. I was delighted. Finally, a brother! Then I got drunk in his honor.

Even Brendan O'Connor lectured me. "Patrick, what are you doing? You're hanging around the wrong people. You're losing yourself."

I nodded, not listening, as usual. Because I didn't care, Brendan and I began to drift apart. I also didn't care much about the donkeys anymore—it was almost like they were invisible to me. I didn't spend much time up at the rock either. It was still there, waiting back at the center of my world, but I was like a wild donkey running off into the woods, kicking up my heels and leaving paradise behind in the dust. Eden always has a resident serpent, right? Mine had been lying in wait at the bottom of a sherry bottle, and unfortunately, I'd taken it in.

CHAPTER SIX

A WILD DONKEY OF A MAN

❖

This son of yours will be a wild man, as untamed as a wild donkey!
He will raise his fist against everyone, and everyone will be against him.

GENESIS 16:12, NLT

A BEAUTIFUL MULE GLIDING THROUGH the middle of a Dublin slum is a very strange sight. Her name was Jerusalem, and being a mule meant she was half horse, half donkey.

Mules and donkeys don't really belong in cities. Even if they are working animals, they need time out in the fields to graze, which they do for more than half the day if given the chance. Not only do they eat grass, but donkeys also nibble on leaves and seeds from bushes and trees and sometimes chew bark from tree trunks too. They don't need much water, though, as a drink every two or three days will do. Wild donkeys find watering holes or rivers when they are thirsty, and if those dry up, they dig down with their hooves and find their own fresh water underground.

So Jerusalem was already at risk for a short and unhappy life.

Not only was she in a bad part of the city, but she was alone, a hybrid, without any of her own kind. Her environment was dangerous. Shootings, drug deals, pollution, noise, and stress of all kinds were her day-to-day experience.

Dublin is the capital of the Republic of Ireland, and the rows of deteriorating high-rise flats in Jerusalem's neighborhood had been notorious for more than a hundred years, with politicians always talking about cleaning up neighborhoods and enforcing codes with the landlords so people have a decent and safe place to live. But there's also been plenty of corruption and sometimes revelations that the politicians themselves have profited from the misery of the people who live there.

I was working at the donkey sanctuary after bouncing around several different schools due to my behavior. The message was starting to become clear: *Don't come back.*

I needed a job and asked my dad to give me one more chance because it was convenient, not out of any particular sense of mission. I could walk out the back door of our house and go to work, no training needed since I knew how to do the work well. I did my chores to help the donkeys, but more and more they were just part of the landscape, no longer the buddies and soul friends that Aran and Timmy had been to me. Taking care of the donkeys was just a job while I waited for weekends in the pubs and hoped for something better to come along.

A call came in about a mule in Dublin, and when I found out it was in a rough area called Finglas, I was surprised. *This is going to be interesting. Will I need the garda?*

Ironically, Finglas had once been an important village with an early Christian monastery founded there in AD 560 by St. Canice, renowned for his learning and bardic skills. He was a missionary who preached the gospel across Ireland and Scotland. But those days were long gone. Now I was going in by myself to find a lone mule and try to get her out of there. A place that was once a haven for the lost was now too dangerous even for a mule.

I had plenty of time to worry on the three-hour drive to Dublin and worried even more as I drove the van through the dark streets between crumbling buildings, swerving around burned-out cars and stray dogs. I had a phone number, so I pulled over on the right block, made sure my doors were locked, and called. A man with a thick Dublin accent answered and made me even more nervous. I asked him about Jerusalem, and all he said was, "Okay. I'll be down to you in a minute."

I sat and waited. I looked around and there was not a blade of grass to be seen anywhere. There was also no mule. Where was she? And was I in trouble? What had I gotten myself into?

But a few minutes later, there she came, so light on her feet. Jerusalem was a tall, beautiful chestnut mule with a coat that gleamed a rich reddish bronze. Her eyes were shiny and alert, and her ears turned back and forth individually, monitoring the sounds in a relaxed way as if she were very comfortable. She moved with grace, picking up her legs with strength and delicacy, like a ballet dancer going for a stroll through Hades.

Two men came with her, one holding on to a piece of rope attached to her halter. Both men looked rough, probably in their late twenties, and one had a scar on his face. But Jerusalem seemed very much at ease with them. They almost acted like they were . . . friends.

It was such an odd sight—the two men looked like they belonged there, and Jerusalem, a precious jewel, did not.

The men gave me a quick nod, and we walked together to the back of the horse box. The one with the scar said, "Look, can we spend five minutes with her?"

I was surprised. I wanted to get out of there as fast as possible, but I remembered Aran and wondered if they had that kind of connection with Jerusalem.

"No problem." I nodded and turned away, walking to the front of the van to wait.

After a few minutes, I heard them open the door to the horse box and the van shook a bit as Jerusalem climbed up the ramp and inside. Then the door closed with a clunk, and I heard them fasten the latch and give it a shake to make sure it was secure.

I turned around as they approached up the side. Both men were crying, eyes red and brimming with tears. The one with the scar wiped at his eyes and then rubbed his hand on the side of his trousers.

"We had her since we were twelve years old. We bought her at the market in Dublin and taught her how to pull a cart. She took to it right away and always knew what we wanted her to do. And we never tried to make money off her." They looked so sad, like they were saying goodbye to a family member.

We talked for a few more minutes. The reason they had called the sanctuary is because they'd realized the chaotic environment wasn't a great life for Jerusalem. More and more children growing up in that area didn't respect the animals, and they had been teasing Jerusalem and throwing stones at her. The men couldn't afford to leave the city themselves, but they could find a better home for Jerusalem—a place where she could have a better future.

I got in the van and watched the men in the mirrors as I slowly drove away, anxious to get back to my corner of Ireland. I felt like it was the death of a dream for them, but their selfless act meant the beginning of a new life for Jerusalem. She was coming out of a turbulent and troubled environment, but strangely enough she'd been raised with love, respect, and friendship, and she had survived. She had never known better, but I was excited and grateful that she was about to come home to Liscarroll and the haven my parents had created. Her name means "city of peace," and that was my hope for her.

While Jerusalem was about to enter paradise, I was already on my way out. In part it was my own decision, but in part it felt like I was expelled from my village and country, just like I'd been from school.

As a last-ditch effort, my parents sent me to a boarding school. The level of punishment was severe. If you did anything wrong, a priest got you out of bed in the middle of the night and made you stand on the cold marble floor all night long in nothing but boxer shorts. It happened to me more than once and scared me to death—sometimes I was alone, sometimes I was with three or four other lads. It was almost as bad as getting beaten by the headmaster.

I learned to drive and loved the freedom of going where I wanted, but I couldn't handle it. I started crashing cars and getting into trouble at the pubs. Occasionally, if forced, I helped with the work around the sanctuary, but I tried to avoid it if I could, preferring to spend my time holding court in the pubs.

Mam didn't know what to do with me—none of her three daughters had behaved like this—and I wouldn't have listened to her or my sisters anyway. Every once in a while she'd give me a warning. "Watch that drinking. It's no good for ya," she'd say.

Dad walked the halls of the house and prayed the Rosary for me at night when I was out. In the mornings, Mam walked up to the rock and prayed. Maybe she felt the same sense of peace I did when I used to go up there with Aran, but I was too busy to get up there much anymore.

One day Brendan introduced me to a girl named Anita. She was pretty, with long dark hair, hazel eyes, and a fair complexion. She loved animals, especially horses, and was quiet but funny. I felt a genuine connection, like she really cared about me. "You're a real gentle soul," she said to me once. But like Mam, she gave me a hard time about my drinking.

Anita was a talented singer and songwriter. She and her sister, Niamh, had formed a band called Nivita, and they were working on an album called "Attraction, Emotion, and Devotion." We started dating, and it was the first time I dropped my chameleon act and shared some of my thoughts and feelings with a girl.

But I couldn't promise her a future. I didn't know where I was headed. I had no real plans or purpose, and she did. Part of me hoped for a life together some day, but part of me felt like she was better off without me. Plus, she was in the way of the madness of my drinking, so in the end I sabotaged the relationship.

I'd started to create my own reality, telling myself a story of my own making that didn't make much sense to anyone but me. I told myself I was having a great time and not taking anything too seriously, spending time with my friends and making them laugh, and finding my own way. Sports, family, friends, faith, and the donkeys receded into the background of my day-to-day life.

Finally, I was left with only one possibility for the future—the army. I wanted to see what it was like to fly in an airplane and travel to new places; I had a romantic view of army service, equating it with the great warrior myths of Ireland and my rich fantasy life around Liscarroll Castle. Plus, I didn't see myself going any further with my education. I felt suffocated by working at home with the donkeys and living with my parents, and I wanted to get away from it all. So Dad drove me to a recruiting office in Cork City and I picked up an application, filled it out at home, then posted it myself.

While I waited on the army, my focus was on pubs and drinking sessions. Telling long, exaggerated stories punctuated with the occasional barnyard joke or donkey call to my audience in the pubs was the main storyline of my life now—until I got hauled before a judge for something that happened at a funeral.

We take our funerals seriously in Ireland; they are multi-day affairs involving the entire village. Funerals are a time of both mourning and celebration, with a twenty-four-hour wake the first night. The body lies in a coffin in the house while people gather to eat, drink, share their memories with each other, and honor the dead. The next day is a removal ceremony from the house. The third day is the funeral, with solemn processions into and out of the church and then to the graveyard, followed by a final wake with more food and alcohol, crying, laughter, blessings, and memories.

Funerals are an event every bit as important, momentous, and heavily attended as a wedding or birth, and sometimes it's the only time when big Irish families all get together in the same place. So when I accidentally ruined a local funeral, it didn't go well for me.

I regularly made the rounds of all the pubs within a forty-mile radius of Liscarroll. There were nights I didn't come home, and Dad would get worried and start driving around to find me. He could never actually get me home, so I was forced to go farther and farther afield to stay out of his reach. I'd have a few drinks at one pub, then move on to another before the publican got mad at me for mouthing off some sort of nonsense or trying to start a fight.

On this summer day, I'd been out pub hopping in my shiny black Opel Kadett since about ten in the morning with my friend, a good lad named Connie from Liscarroll. We'd finally ended up early that evening in Ballyclough because I wanted to brag about my team beating their village in the hurling finals the weekend before. At first there was a bit of lighthearted banter, then the Ballyclough lads began to act a little sore about the loss (which I enjoyed). As I got progressively more drunk, I began to feel like they were trying to get me drunk and into trouble (the story I was telling myself). So I got angry. The truth of it was I wanted attention—either positive or negative, I didn't care which—and went there looking for it. The lads in the pub got angry back at me and I stormed out, ready for a spot of trouble.

That's a good picture of the pub life. It seems happy and fun-loving on the surface, but there is plenty of misery underneath. "Street angel, house devil," Mam used to say, shaking her head whenever I went Jekyll and Hyde on her. Mam didn't drink, following the example of both her parents who had taken the Pioneer Pledge of abstinence from alcohol at their confirmation in the Catholic church. My grandfather always wore his Pioneer pin proudly to mass.

By the time I emerged from the pub, it was 7:30 p.m. and still daylight, and Connie and I took off driving at top speed. On a byroad coming out of Ballyclough, Connie and I started arguing over the radio station. The arguing turned to drunken shouting, and we started throwing fists at each other. Then, something made me look up. We were zooming upwards of 70 kilometers per hour down a narrow stretch of road with cars parked on both sides.

Suddenly I lost control of the car and veered to the side to hit one car, then bounced off and skidded across the road to hit a car on the opposite side, then back across the road like a pinball and crashed into a third car—a big black hearse with a coffin inside. Family members had been standing around talking on the front walk, but somehow no one was hit.

The impact with the hearse caused my car to flip over at least twice and come to rest upside down in the middle of the road.

I was so drunk I didn't know what had happened. I didn't feel shaken up, just confused.

"What were ye doing?" someone shouted, as people pulled me from the car.

"Are you all right?" someone else asked, staring at the blood trickling down my face.

We hadn't bothered to put on our seatbelts when we got in the car, and somehow I'd gripped the steering wheel and held on as tight as I could without being thrown from the car. But Connie went through the windscreen headfirst, hitting the rearview mirror on his way out. He didn't have any major injuries, but a few days later, a bruise in the exact shape of the mirror covered his face. The bruise resembled a mask, and I called Connie "Zorro." We were both fine and back in the pubs later that night in Liscarroll, drinking and telling stories. To us, everything was grand.

That's the part of the story I embellished, regaling listeners in the pubs.

But here's the true story: I risked my life getting in that car and driving. I don't know how I did not die.

I risked Connie's life. He wasn't wearing a seatbelt, he was riding with a drunk, and he was in a potentially lethal car crash with someone who had a history of car crashes.

I wrecked or damaged the cars of three innocent people.

If anyone had been on the road, I could have killed them.

I traumatized the people who either witnessed the accident or came to help us after the crash.

And here's the worst—the last car I hit, the big black hearse, was parked outside the house of the man who had died. The cars were lined up along the street because people were there for the removal service, and he was in the coffin inside the hearse. So his children witnessed me crashing into the hearse that held their father's body.

What a nightmare for them all. Yet to me, at the time, it was a good pub story.

I did have to go to the hospital to get checked out. The police followed me there and wanted to test my blood alcohol level, but right after the accident—before the police arrived—a man had come out from one of the houses with a bottle of brandy and quickly poured some down my throat.

"There's no Breathalyzing this lad," the neighbor told the garda at the scene. "He's had some brandy for shock."

When I got to the hospital to have my scrapes cleaned up, the doctors sent the police away. With that amount of alcohol in my system, if I'd been tested, the results would have sent me straight to jail.

While I didn't face charges for drunken driving, I was hauled in front of a judge at the courthouse in Mallow for reckless driving. The judge was a heavyset man with a round bald head, a beard, and a frown. I had enough sense to be scared; I'd heard of his fearsome reputation. My dad was there with me, and the judge looked at him, then at me, and gave me a choice: follow through with enlisting in the Irish army (where I would likely ship out to the Middle East) or go to jail.

The judge looked down at me. "This can be a new start for you."

I wasn't excited, exactly. I'd already had a few new starts with changing schools, but this *would* be a big new start. I followed through and looked forward to leaving the village and seeing the world.

I got off with a small fine and the promise of adventure and possibly a career in the army. I'd always wanted to be a soldier. Maybe it was time to see if I could embark on this new path and learn how to make my family proud.

Liscarroll was well-known for its stubborn sense of independence. Our castle changed hands several times in battles and a thirteen-day siege in the 1600s. During the Irish War of Independence in the early 1900s, Liscarroll Castle was used as a military outpost for the British army but soon was reclaimed by the Irish Republican Army (IRA), who moved in and destroyed the fortifications made by the British military. When the British came back to the castle in 1921, the IRA conducted a raid and opened fire on their enemy with rifles and later added grenades to the mix. There were no casualties, but the British abandoned the castle and took over the school.

During the War of Independence, men of the village fought bravely, led by revolutionary hero Paddy O'Brien, whose son still operates O'Brien's Pub in Liscarroll. Paddy's British Enfield rifle, with scars on the wood, hangs there on the wall. In an upstairs room at the pub, Paddy and his fellow freedom fighters met and made plans to defend our village and the surrounding areas from the Black and Tans (named for the colors of the British uniforms).

Growing up, I heard about Sean Moylan, Tom Kelliher, Daniel O'Brien, and Dan Murphy, brave volunteers who died in the war effort and fought against a better-armed British military so we could have our freedom. These were big boots to fill, and I hoped I was up to the challenge.

Dad and my sisters were quiet about it, and Mam didn't cry or show much emotion during my initial stints of military training before I left for the Middle East, either. Instead, she made sure I had all of the clothes and supplies I needed, including plenty of fresh, clean boxers and socks. She packed up food, bits of sausage and tea biscuits, so I'd have something to eat on the way. I was the baby of the family but the first to leave the country, and she must have been suffering from worry, though she didn't show it. She'd been through worse.

The night before I shipped out to Beirut, Mam knew I was upset, and she came to sit on the bed next to me. We sat quietly side by side, Mam worried about her wayward son and me hungover. She tapped my leg. "Everything is going to be okay.

Remember to keep your head down, Patrick. Just keep your head down now."

I looked at Mam, blonde hair shining and wavy around her face. She smiled a little, but her blue eyes were sad. It hit me then—I wasn't going to be seeing my mam and dad or my sisters or Anita for a very long time. I wouldn't be seeing the castle or the hills around Liscarroll or the donkeys. *Will they miss me?*

It had been something of a celebration over the last week, with plenty of time in the pubs. A lad going away to serve meant a big celebration, and everyone knew they could find me on a stool in the pubs, so they came to say goodbye. Anita and I had officially broken up, but when I was getting ready to leave, I'd driven to her house for one more moment together. We talked on the porch for a while. "Patrick, you mind yourself," she said before walking me out to my car.

She called out, "See you later," but I didn't bother to turn around. Instead, I climbed into my car and drove off with a quick wave. There was still something between us, and I felt uneasy, like we had unfinished business. *Am I running away?*

I took along a picture of the village and the castle taken from the rock at the top of the sanctuary, with the rolling green fields stretched out all around. Whenever I looked at it, I could feel the cool air on my face, smell the rich green grass, and hear the songs of the donkeys. I felt exactly like Jerusalem—plucked from my natural home and soon to be dropped into a new place where I surely didn't belong.

Would I be back? I wondered. I didn't know what was ahead, but I couldn't go back, only forward. I pictured Jerusalem again, walking down the dark street with courage and grace, headed for paradise. Maybe there was hope for me. *Maybe someday I'll be like Jerusalem.*

CHAPTER SEVEN

VALENTINE'S DAY

❖

We come bulletproof in Ireland.
We're reared tough, and we fight.

CONOR MCGREGOR

AT FIRST I loved the military life. Before we shipped out to Beirut, we trained in the Galtee Mountains, and it was exciting to be training out in the forest like Paddy O'Brien and the other Liscarroll soldiers would have done. We marched through pine forests filled with wild stag and slept in one-man tents next to clear streams tumbling over waterfalls into icy pools. I loved the drills, meeting the physical challenges with ease, and learning how to properly handle real weapons with the other lads. It almost felt like a vacation.

One afternoon my company of forty soldiers marched out in the woods on a survival exercise called "escape and evade" and were given some crates of live chickens to prepare for dinner. I took the opportunity to jog to the market several kilometers away and came back with cigarettes and chocolate, expecting to smell chicken roasting over the fire when I returned. Not so. The city boys in my company were still trying to figure out how to kill the chickens, so I took over and did the deed. Being a farm boy was turning out to be an advantage in certain ways I hadn't anticipated. As our training continued, I relaxed a little and started to enjoy being part of a team.

Soon enough, it was October and time to leave Ireland for Beirut. I was later told the day my unit left for Lebanon, Anita was at a café, and when the Celine Dion song "Because You Loved Me" came on, she thought of me. She called the house and talked to Mam, who told her I was on my way to the Dublin Airport. Anita rang the airport to try and catch me.

I was sitting on the airport shuttle bus with a lad named Martin Ormond, nicknamed Fraggle, waiting until we could get on our transport plane. Just then, our commander stepped through the door and called out, "Trooper Barrett, there's a phone call for you in the airport. A girl by the name of Anita."

I looked at Fraggle and shrugged, a little embarrassed to be singled out this way. Then I made a decision. "It's okay, sir. I'll call her back when I get to Lebanon." *I'll have plenty of time to call her when I get there.*

❖⸺◉ ◉⸺❖

After an uneventful flight, we landed in Beirut, a five-thousand-year-old city on the Mediterranean coast that had once been an elegant and sophisticated jewel of a city. Once the banking capital of the Middle East, flush with oil money and a rich cultural life, the city was now recovering from a complex civil war that had cost 150,000 lives and upended the residents' lives with street violence, sieges, kidnappings, murders, and generalized terror and chaos.

You could say the entire region suffered from post-traumatic stress disorder (PTSD) after what they had been through.

Since 1978, the Irish Army had sent tens of thousands of soldiers into Lebanon as part of the United Nations Interim Force in Lebanon (UNIFIL). Our job would be to supervise, observe, and prevent fighting between Israel and a well-funded terrorist group called Hezbollah. I was part of the 86th Battalion Mobile Reserve (BMR), an all-purpose unit with many responsibilities—protecting the infantry, sweeping for mines, serving as ambulance crews, patrolling in armored cars, cleaning up after violence, and providing humanitarian aid for the locals.

We came freshly trained, fully armed, and ready (or so we thought) to serve in a war zone. I put on a brave front, but inside I already felt a little bit like the runaway bunny from the classic children's book. In it, a brash little bunny wants to run away from his home and family, but he has no clue what he's getting himself into. Lucky for him, his mam saves him.

An army bus met us at the airport to take us to our base up in the hills. I sat by a chap from County Cavan named Barney Mulligan. This was his thirteenth trip to Lebanon. Barney sensed my nervousness at being so far away from home in a war-torn place, so he started a conversation.

"Young Barrett, how old are ye now?"

"I'm nineteen going on twenty."

"Barrett, did you ever hear of the Dead Sea?"

"Yes, I have." I thought maybe he was about to disclose some insider stories from his deployment to help me acclimate.

"Well, I remember when the Dead Sea was still sick!"

That was just the first in a string of silly jokes Barney had for me. The Irish love a good pun.

Jokes aside, guerrilla warfare was still taking place and my cavalry unit patrolled nightly in vintage French-made tanks, rolling past dusty bunkers and shelled-out ruins of buildings. The French troops laughed at us, saying our equipment was so old they'd seen it displayed in a Paris museum. It was all we had, though, to protect us from terrorist attacks. Irish soldiers had been caught, tortured, and killed by the South Lebanese Army (SLA), a Lebanese Christian–dominated militia backed by the Israelis against Muslims. We wore khaki uniforms with an embroidered UN badge on the left shoulder and an Irish flag patch on the right, blue flak jackets and helmets when on patrol, and we carried big guns over our shoulders.

It was a religious war and the atmosphere in this militarized zone was more than tense. I lived in a constant state of adrenaline even on a routine patrol. It made me feel very much alive, but it was hard to turn off.

Another problem I faced in both training and deployment was the drinking culture. I'm not sure if it was better or worse than what I left behind, but alcohol seemed to be a big part of the soldier's life. There was nothing much to do in the basic rooms we inhabited in our boxy building, so we often headed to local bars when off duty. At one point I met an Irish lad named Bob, and I liked to sit with him. Bob made me feel comfortable. I noticed he didn't drink at all, though, and he seemed at peace. How could he be here in this mess and not drink? It made no sense to me.

One night, Bob looked me in the eye. "You'll have to watch what you're doing."

Why is he talking to me like that? This is weird. I was taken aback by what seemed like a stern warning from someone I hadn't known that long.

"It's going to catch up with you," he continued. "If you keep going the way you're going, you're going to be in trouble."

I brushed it off at the time because I didn't see a problem. I felt fine just the way I was. But I never forgot his words. They carried truth, and the power of that truth, spoken to me by someone who cared, seemed to work down into the cracks of my soul. It hadn't taken Bob long to see right through me. For a brief moment, I remembered the nightmares I had as a boy of Jesus facing off against the devil in the desert, and I felt a quick chill.

⟡ ⟡

I'd only been in Lebanon for a week when Captain MacNamara singled me out one afternoon when I got back from a patrol. The captain had a kindness as well as a sense of strength about her, and she was much respected.

"Barrett, get over here." I could tell by her voice that something was wrong.

Is it my grandmother? I wondered. Maybe something had happened to Mam's mother, who wasn't in good health. I couldn't think of what else it could be.

I jogged over to the captain's office. Her expression was serious, and my gut clenched up in a knot before she even told me the news. It wasn't my grandmother; it was Anita. She was dead, killed in a car crash the day before. She was just seventeen years old.

At first I didn't know what to feel. I ran to my room in shock and slammed the door. Fraggle and some of the other guys banged on the door to see if I was okay, but I had no idea if I was. Some kind of dark place had opened up inside of me, and part of me got lost there. *Anita is gone.* I couldn't believe it.

Then it hit me. *I never called her back.* I had tried once on the satellite phone and actually heard her voice on the line, but the connection was poor and she couldn't hear me, so I had given up.

I had no money to get home and couldn't think how to make it happen, but a bunch of the lads pooled their money together and surprised me with a plane ticket back to Ireland for Anita's funeral.

It was surreal retreating from a war zone to go back home to the peace of the village and the donkey sanctuary.

⊶⊷

When I got home, I learned more details about the car accident. Anita, her sister Niamh, and a friend named Carmel with her baby, Emma, had been driving in Charleville, a nearby town, when their car was hit head-on by a car traveling on the wrong side of the road. The impact had caused their car to flip over the barrier and into a field, where they landed upside down. All four of them perished.

I didn't get back to Liscarroll in time for the removal ceremony, but the following day I was able to attend the funeral for all of them at the church. I sat with my friend Brendan.

Before mass, Anita's oldest sister, Karen, called to me, "Patrick, do you want to see Anita before she goes?"

I was sitting in the middle of the church and afraid to go up there by myself and said the only thing I could think of. "She would want me to remember her the way she was." Karen gave me a sad smile and seemed to understand.

The mood was somber, and I was overwhelmed. I couldn't tell you what was said or who was there; I was too numb to cry and just sat there in a daze, staring at the coffins up front. After the service, the coffins were closed, and I went up with the other pallbearers to help carry Anita's coffin out to the hearse.

At the wake, Anita's best friend, Lisa, handed me a sealed envelope with my name written on the front. I took it, looked down at Anita's handwriting, and felt a wave of something—Confusion? Grief? Loss?—shoot through my body like an electric charge.

"She was going to mail it to you," said Lisa.

I don't remember when I actually opened the letter, but I know it was sometime later that day when I got back to Mam and Dad's after a few drinks. When I tore open the envelope, I felt like I was in a dream. The letter inside was dated the night before Anita died, and it was a goodbye letter. I don't remember her exact words, but she had a feeling I might not make it back from Lebanon. Several times in the letter, in different ways, she told me again to mind myself. "Don't be too brave," she wrote, "and keep your head down."

I was stunned. *Did she know something bad was going to happen?* Her words inferred she thought something was going to happen to *me*. The realization of the loss of this dear friend hit me harder than ever, like part of me had died in that car along with her. I would never see her again on this earth.

I went out drinking that night, and the next day I was at Mam and Dad's, dealing with a massive hangover from the night before. I decided to take a walk around the sanctuary, and out of habit I found myself at the rock, up on the hill. I hadn't expected to be back there again so soon. It was a little rainy and misty, and I watched the donkeys in the field below huddle together under the low-hanging branches of a tree like old ladies underneath a giant leafy umbrella. The herd stuck together and kept each other warm and comforted.

Even though they live in herds, a donkey will often develop a close bonded relationship with another donkey, and the two become what the Irish call "soul friends." In Irish, *anam* is soul, and *cara* is friend. An *anam cara* is someone you can share your innermost soul with. They will be honest with you, love you, and always stick by you. It's a joining up in an ancient and eternal way that goes beyond a typical friendship.

When two donkeys partner up like this, they have a difficult time when one of them dies or is taken away. It's not unusual for the remaining donkey to get depressed, stop eating, and develop a physical condition called *hypolipemia*. Sometimes a new friend helps, but if not, the remaining donkey often dies within six months to a year after his or her partner is gone.

I had lost a true friend, and I felt a little like one of those grieving donkeys. But I didn't want to think about it too much. I wanted to keep it together and stay in control of my emotions. I decided I needed to rejoin *my* herd, so I took myself back down the hill and headed off to the carefree laughter, camaraderie, and liquid warmth of my favorite place on the planet—the pub.

As the sun shone through the mist, a massive rainbow arced across the sky, but I barely noticed it. I hadn't stayed long enough at the rock to find comfort or peace. Instead, I stayed in Liscarroll for a week, went out every night and drank as much as I could to get through it all, then flew back to Lebanon.

⟿ ⟾

As soon as I returned to my unit, I went right back to patrols. My cavalry unit patrolled the outposts for several companies, checking for land mines on the main roads. We moved artillery around, escorted a mobile armored ambulance as needed, and helped mop up after Hezbollah attacks. This was gruesome work and sometimes involved cleaning up after violent attacks on the locals. We were on call and anything could—and did—happen. To do this I had to disengage from reality; if I pretended I was playing a part in a movie, I could function better and keep my head quiet . . . at least until I got back to base. But with the constant threat of attack, we all functioned in a state of hypervigilance when we were out on patrol, and this mental state was hard to shift out of. Alcohol helped.

Most of the time I felt like I was thriving in this adrenaline-laced environment, and the intensity kept me from thinking too much about what had happened to Anita and everyone else I'd left behind. I switched myself off so much that I stopped communicating with my parents. When they hadn't heard from me in weeks, they were worried and contacted the barracks to see if I was okay. My detail officer had to order me to call them back.

I spent Christmas in Lebanon, although I have no memory of it. The next date I remember at all is Valentine's Day 2000, when a bunch of us were preparing to go on leave to Thailand, excited for a break from the war zone. It was just three months after Anita's death, and I felt like I was just starting to come to terms with the loss. I looked forward to a little slice of heaven with sunshine, good food and drinks, and relaxing.

I threw some clothes into a bag and jogged over to headquarters to get a seat in the convoy. About two dozen men were gathered, waiting for a ride down the mountain. Excitement was in the air, with friends meeting up and trying to ride together. We planned to spend the night at a hotel in Beirut and then fly out the next day.

I was waiting my turn to get in a Jeep when Fraggle came alongside. We were the last two standing—everyone else had already found a seat. A Jeep with a canvas top over the back looked like it had room, so we walked over and saw some lads we knew from Company B in the back.

"Is there room for us?" I asked John Paul, a chap from my unit who was sitting in the cab.

There were five guys in the back, and since I thought we could squeeze in, I threw in my bag and started climbing in, then sat straddled on the tailgate talking to them. I knew these lads from a quick three-day trip we'd just taken to the Holy Land and was trying to talk my way in.

Fraggle wandered over and repeated the question: "Is there room?"

"Where are ye going?" they asked.

"Thailand," I smiled big. "How about you?"

"We're going to meet our girlfriends for Valentine's Day. I'm going to get engaged in Cyprus," one said.

"Why are ye doing that?" I laughed, with a wink.

Just then Fraggle saw a hardtop Jeep from Battalion Mobile Reserve coming around the corner.

"Go find your own Jeep," one of the lads said.

"Fine," I retorted. "I'll go find something right grand." I hopped out to rejoin Fraggle but left my bag with the lads.

"Mind my bag," I called over my shoulder, then jumped into the cab of the hardtop Jeep. The driver was Noel, a lad from another unit with the same rank as me. There was plenty of room, and Fraggle and I settled in for the ride while the lads in the other truck laughed.

The convoy started rolling down the mountain road, on the edge of a cliff overlooking a *wadi*. We were in front of the Jeep with the boys heading to Cyprus. Suddenly, we hit something in the road, causing our truck to give a bit of a kick, and at the same time I saw something spatter on the windscreen. Noel put on the wipers, which didn't help—the droplets smeared and streaked across the glass. "There must have been a fuel spill," Noel said. Whatever it was blended in with the tarmac because we hadn't seen it coming.

Something made me look back, and I watched as the Jeep behind us hit that fuel slick too. The vehicle started sliding back and forth, violently out of control, then suddenly flipped over onto its side, slamming into the metal barrier next to the cliff.

"Stop, stop, stop!" I shouted to Noel. As he hit the brakes hard, Fraggle called for a Medivac on the radio. Fraggle and I jumped out of the cab and ran toward the wreck, then Noel threw the Jeep into reverse, picked us up, did a fast U-turn, and drove us back to the accident. All I could think about was getting to the boys in the back, who had only the Jeep's soft top as protection.

The lads in the cab were banged up, but alive. But out of the five lads in the back, we found only one of them—Eugene O'Neill—on the side of the road. When Eugene started to hurtle out of the back of the Jeep, he'd hit the roll bar and was saved from flying over the cliff. He was on his knees, dazed and bloody, but he was alive.

The other four were nowhere in sight.

"They must have catapulted over the barrier," I shouted at Fraggle. It looked like an eighty-foot drop to the bottom.

Fraggle and I looked at each other in horror and, without thinking too much, kicked into action, jumping over the barrier and scrambling down the side of the cliff like a couple of spiders.

The surface was jagged rock and shale, sharp and unstable. We didn't have a clear plan or orders, and we weren't even sure what had happened. My heart was beating a thousand beats a second and my head felt on fire. I just knew I had to find those boys and save them. I kept shouting, "Get someone down here! Get someone down here!"

Out of the corner of my eye, I saw someone waving us back up. But I didn't want to go back up. I wanted to *do* something. I was out of my head, not thinking, just acting on instinct.

I couldn't save Anita, but maybe I can save one of these guys.

I found one lad, lying to the right of me. I checked his pulse, but he didn't have one, his head injuries too severe.

Down at the bottom I spotted another and moved toward him, hoping to help, but he was gone too. There was nothing to be done for any of them.

Four men dead, and it had all happened in an instant. Nothing had prepared me for this moment, and I couldn't believe what I was seeing. I wasn't going back up without them. I bent down and tried to pull one of the soldiers up, but I knew I would never be able to get even one of them to the top of the cliff.

"What are you doing?" Fraggle's voice was hysterical, but all I could see was these lads, and I just wanted to bring them all home.

We tried, Fraggle, I wanted to shout, but the words stayed inside. *We tried to help them. We were there with them.*

We climbed back up the cliff to a scene of utter chaos, with people running everywhere and emergency vehicles and television trucks not far behind. Fraggle and I tried hard to protect the dignity of our friends below, and we got into a fight, trading some punches with the cameramen. Fraggle threw one television camera to the ground, and lads from the convoy finally dragged us away before we really got into trouble.

They drove us to the Mayflower, a hotel in downtown Beirut, where we had been booked to spend the night before our flights to Thailand the next day. They isolated Fraggle and me in our room, and we weren't allowed to call anyone or have any contact with others while the accident was sorted out. The first thing we did was call room service and order a big pitcher of beer.

While we were drinking the beer in a complete daze, Fraggle looked at me and I looked back at him. His eyes had a haunted look, and I know mine did too.

"I think you'd better change your clothes," he said.

I looked down; I was spattered in blood. He was too.

Then I remembered. *I left my bag in their Jeep. I should have been in there too.*

Fraggle and I kept drinking.

Someone retrieved my bag and dropped it off at the hotel. When I saw the blood on the bag, I didn't even want to touch it.

Late that night I was allowed to call home, and Mam answered the phone. She'd heard about the accident on the local news, and my parents hadn't known if I was dead or alive.

She listened quietly and calmly as I told her what had happened. She was good and steady in an emergency. Just hearing Mam's quiet-but-strong voice comforted me, the same voice she used with the donkeys. She was the glue that held everything around her together, and I wished she were there with me.

I didn't remember much after that. I didn't even remember much of the climb down the cliff or the details of what I saw. I blocked it all out. But I *did* remember I originally had been in the back of that Jeep. I was supposed to die. I would have died if one of those lads hadn't kicked me out, or if Fraggle hadn't called me to the other Jeep. I couldn't wrap my mind around any of it. It didn't make any sense, and I knew it probably never would.

But I knew what to do to feel better. I knew what to do to numb and depress my feelings and painful memories. I'd been drinking for more than a decade by then, and it was my go-to for any situation where there was any kind of pain or discomfort, whether physical, emotional, or spiritual. The drink hadn't failed me yet. Or at least I kept telling myself that.

I stubbornly kept on doing what I'd always done, even though it had already cost me plenty.

Donkeys are stubborn, too, but they act stubborn in order to preserve their lives. I still had a lot to learn from them.

CHAPTER EIGHT

PENELOPE
AND PEANUT

⊕

Let me tell you this: if you meet a loner, no matter what they tell you,
it's not because they enjoy solitude.
It's because they have tried to blend into the world before,
and people continue to disappoint them.

JODI PICOULT, *My Sister's Keeper*

PENELOPE AND PEANUT were two odd little creatures who were brought to the donkey sanctuary. These two weren't donkeys—they were Shetland ponies—but I'm here to testify that they were as intelligent, stubborn, and willful as donkeys!

Shetland ponies originated in the Shetland Isles off the coast of Scotland, and they are easy to spot because they are tiny and very furry. They get even furrier in winter and resemble a big ball of fuzzy brown twine sitting on short stubby legs, with big brown eyes peering out from beneath unruly, frizzy bangs.

But like donkeys, Shetland ponies have their own strong opinions and can be very determined. They're also powerful and sturdy like donkeys, so they have long been used to pull carts, haul peat and coal, and even plow farmland. They're hardy and their coarse, thick coats keep them warm.

Children love Shetlands because the ponies are their size and look like the perfect pet. But an adult can't ride them, so training them is a problem. A child needs to be as stubborn and strong-willed as the pony to make the animal behave and not buck or run off like a wild mustang.

Enter Penelope and Peanut, a mother and son that Dad rescued from some horse traders. The two had been used exclusively for breeding, with no attempt to gentle them or teach them manners. The pair were rarely handled and had no affection from people at all. Penelope and Peanut were not pets and had not been taught to pull a cart. No one could ride them for fear of dying prematurely. Sadly, Penelope's whole purpose in life had been to undergo forced breeding and to remain pregnant as often as possible, in order to produce as many foals as possible so her offspring could be sold at the horse fairs to families looking for a pony for their children.

Because of this rather limited experience with the outside world, Penelope and Peanut viewed all humans with extreme suspicion and, shall we say, a measure of outright hostility. They had no use for people whatsoever. They both showed their feelings whenever they could by giving a nip on the elbow if you happened to get too close. I quickly learned to give Penelope as much space as she wanted.

We tried everything to help them learn to love us, or like us, or at least tolerate us. Patience is always important when trying to care for a mistreated or neglected animal, so that was the first rule. After that, feeding and caring for them usually works well. So do treats like carrots or apples. When a new rescue relaxes a bit, a little scratching of the withers, donkey-style, is always appreciated. All of this takes time—lots of time.

But in the peculiar case of Penelope and Peanut, none of these approaches worked. We tried everything we could think of. This pair of curmudgeons preferred being on their own and were kept by themselves in a stall at the far end of the row in the barn. They didn't cooperate with crucial veterinary or dental procedures or farrier work, which made caring for them difficult. Everything was a struggle and potentially dangerous, and we ended up having to sedate them to perform any procedures on them.

Finally, after months of effort, I gave up on trying to be their friend. Would Penelope and Peanut even accept new friends? Mam, Helen, and I decided to try moving them into different pastures with donkeys and mules to see what would happen. Would the donkeys accept these oddballs into the herd? If the donkeys wouldn't, would the mules? Or would there be disagreements, fights, and perhaps even serious injuries? It wasn't practical or healthy to keep Penelope and Peanut in solitary confinement for the rest of their lives. Herd animals do best in a herd, but these two were antisocial to the core.

Finally, there was a breakthrough. For some reason, Penelope took to the mules. At first she and Peanut began grazing near the mules, all of them facing the same direction but spread apart. Those spaces got smaller and smaller, and in a matter of weeks the mules had adopted the two misfits into their herd, and they were one big happy family.

One memorable mule in Penelope's new herd was Tootsie, who had a very strange overbite. His teeth were so long they looked curly. While he wasn't too attractive, he was quite hardy and eventually became the world's oldest mule, living to the ripe old age of fifty-six.

Because mules are genetically half horse, they are usually flightier and more temperamental than donkeys, and this seemed to appeal to Penelope's inner crotchety old lady. Maybe she saw herself as the caretaker of these hybrids or the serious schoolmaster who needed to keep them in line, or maybe she just enjoyed their antics. Whatever the reason, Penelope decided she and Peanut belonged with the mules, and she adopted them as her own herd. Everyone at the sanctuary breathed a sigh of relief. Penelope and Peanut had found their tribe.

The funny thing is that mules are taller than most donkeys, so they towered above Penelope. She didn't care. She'd chosen them, they had accepted her, and eventually the pony duo ended up settling happily into a big mule farm in England that is part of the Donkey Sanctuary international charity. To this day, Penelope and Peanut still don't like humans.

I was so happy when I heard that Penelope and Peanut were no longer lonely and had found their herd, but I still needed to find mine. I wanted to find someone, the person who wanted to be with me, the real me. I knew my *anam cara* was out there waiting for me somewhere. But I didn't know where she was or where to look.

Most often, I turned to the pubs, whether I was on leave in Liscarroll or back on active duty in Lebanon. My first priority was always the drink, but I also kept an eye out for my soulmate. Believe it or not, even though I spent a lot of time inebriated, for the most part going to the pubs in Ireland is not about getting drunk. For hundreds of years the pubs have been one of the centers of village life, the place where you drop in every day to find out what is going on with your neighbors and how everybody feels about it. You can talk about the latest in sports, politics, or the rising price of petrol.

Dad would usually drop by one of the pubs in Liscarroll on Fridays, Saturdays, and Sundays to meet with friends after work. Some people, often the farmers who lived and worked locally, went every day.

When we kids went to the pubs with Dad on Saturday or Sunday, it was a highlight of the week because there were sure to be other kids there. Dad would buy each of my sisters and me a big bottle of Coca-Cola and bags of Tatos crisps. Mam would drink sparkling apple juice or a Club Orange soda. The place was packed with couples young and old, large extended families, and out-of-town visitors—going to the pub was a part of Irish life, like brushing your teeth or combing your hair. On special occasions there was live music and singing, with everyone joining in. "The Walls of Liscarroll" was always requested, with musicians playing the jig on a fiddle or two, a tin whistle, or even a banjo. And, of course, there were plenty of stories shared.

I've heard so many stories, I can't remember the half of them and, to be honest, sometimes I had too much drink in me to remember what I heard. But I'll never forget one about Michael Flatley, the *Riverdance* creator and step dance performer, who made himself a pot of gold with his stage shows featuring Irish music and dance.

After he had become very successful, Flatley (or Flatfoot as some have called him) began spending time in Irish villages and purchased a large manor house in County Cork called Castlehyde to use as a vacation home for his family. The house is about 35,000 square feet, so he had plenty of room to practice his dancing.

Near his home is a small village called Ballyhooly, with a pub called Griddle's that Michael began to frequent when he was in town. Griddle's is ancient, dusty, and cluttered, and looks like an old attic full of centuries of stuff. Locals purchased their drinks in cans or bottles because they didn't trust that there was a clean glass to be found in the place.

One day after a hard day of dancing, Michael went to Griddle's. He was wearing a fine custom-made coat that he took off and threw onto what looked like another coat on a bench by the window. Then he turned to old man Griddle.

"Give me a pint of your finest Guinness," he said, sitting down for some authentic *craic*, where he could set his fame aside for a moment and mix in with the locals.

Just then something stirred under Michael's expensive coat on the bench, rose up, and started growling.

Michael spun around, straining to see what was going on. A dusty, matted old farm dog that had been asleep on the bench was fiercely mauling the coat. Since the pub was dimly lit, the dog had blended right in with the surroundings and must have had a fright when Michael threw his coat on top of him.

The old dog valiantly fought for his life . . . and won. Unfortunately, Michael's coat sustained mortal wounds in the battle of the window seat.

The locals watched and felt sorry for poor Michael, whose coat had done nothing to deserve such treatment. But perhaps they knew he could afford a new coat, maybe even an upgrade, so it wasn't as tragic as it could have been. The unfortunate incident didn't deter Flatley from returning to Griddle's often after that fateful day.

Another pub story I never got tired of telling was the one about English actor Oliver Reed, who lived in the nearby village of Churchtown. He was legendary for his alcoholism and binge drinking, often becoming angry and aggressive, resulting in bar fights and other kinds of altercations.

One day Reed walked into one of the local pubs, threw a handful of coins on the bar, and shouted, "Buy the peasants a drink."

This didn't go over well.

Sometimes when a fight breaks out in a pub, the locals sit back and let disagreements be sorted out with fists, which is what happened this time. I'm not sure who won, but since Reed had been a boxer before he became an actor, I'm sure he gave out as good as he got.

Another day, I was driving back from a local town called

Buttevant and came upon a black dog in the road. She looked just like Misty, my sister Helen's black Labrador retriever, so I stopped and coaxed her into the car. We drove to Mam and Dad's, and I took Misty into the kitchen. She seemed nervous, though, and was jumping around and couldn't seem to settle down, knocking cushions off the couch in the sitting room and making a mess.

What's going on? This dog has gone mad!

I locked poor Misty up in the kitchen and kept trying to ring Helen. I finally reached her at home.

"Helen, I found Misty and brought her home. There's something wrong with her though. She won't settle down!"

"What are you on about?" Helen said. "Misty is right here in the kitchen looking at me!"

Oops. Did I accidentally kidnap someone's dog?

Just then I heard a loud knock on the door. More like a banging, really. I opened the door, and a big man with long hair and a scruffy gray beard looked at me with blazing blue eyes and shouted in a broad English accent, "Have you seen a black dog!"

It was Oliver Reed. If you've ever seen him in the movie *Gladiator*, you might have a sense of the force of his physical presence and personality in close quarters. Especially when he's angry.

Oliver's dog came running out of the kitchen and started jumping on him in joy. I, on the other hand, was afraid of what was going to happen next.

"What are you doing with my bloody dog?" he said in a quiet voice.

Oops again.

A few days later I saw Reed in a pub. He looked at me and shouted with a certain kind of glee. "Look! There's the bloody bloke who robbed my dog!"

I'm guessing the incident added to my growing reputation.

Being in a pub felt like my home away from home. Where the rock at the top of the sanctuary had once been my anchor and true north, now I'd reset my inner compass to calibrate to the pubs, any pub. I felt like a man when I was there, and the drink and camaraderie and joking made me both command attention and hide in plain sight.

No one knew who I really was anymore, and like Oliver Reed, I'd become an actor in my own life, a pretender who looked like I had it all together. People laughed at my stories and my donkey calls, and I felt strong and brave and a little wild. I played the part of a hell-raiser, and before long, I couldn't separate the role from the actual person I was on the inside. Or maybe that *was* the real me?

Back in Lebanon on my military tours, I was surrounded by people, but even though I was always with my mates and there was plenty of eating and drinking and camaraderie, I felt very alone.

The problem was, I was resilient. I was never one to give up on anything easily, and once I chose a lane, I stayed in it to the end. I used to carry weight on my back during training—upwards of seven stone five pounds (103 pounds) and sometimes even more— and I could keep going thanks to my years roaming the hills with the donkeys. Nothing seemed to break me. I'd get exhausted, but I'd keep going. I'd rather fall down and black out than give up. It takes a lot to break me down and stop me or make me change course.

I was still numb and in pain from the back-to-back deaths of Anita and the lads on Valentine's Day, the day I should have died too. And yet it wasn't enough to make me ask for help or seek to change anything. I lived in a haze of patrols, eating and drinking, and carousing and sleeping. That was about the extent of my life.

I didn't think about God or the meaning of life. If the idea ever crossed my mind, I questioned God for his part in all of this. *Why did you let Anita and the lads die? Why not me?* I didn't hear an answer, so I tried not to think about it. I moved through life like a robot, but I kept going. I wasn't living; I was existing.

For the next few years, I was like Penelope—not letting anyone get close and if they did, giving them a little nudge or bite to encourage them to give me plenty of space. I used to feel like no one could see the real me, but now I didn't *want* anyone to see the real me. I still loved animals because I knew they couldn't hurt me, and I loved my family because they were always there for me, but I had a hard time loving others, and I had an even harder time loving myself.

Maybe not dying on that Valentine's Day gave me something of a death wish. Maybe I considered myself a dead man walking. I don't know, but life became something of a blur. I would serve six months in Lebanon, then go home for a few months' leave. I didn't have any trouble picking up an odd job, doing security work for banks or prisons in larger towns around the area, while still in the service of the Irish Defence Forces. Whenever I came home with money in my pocket, I spent it on cars and drink. I was being paid by the Irish army and received a second paycheck from the UN that I couldn't touch while I was on duty but received in full whenever I went home. Sometimes when I was on leave I drank all day, at pubs all over the countryside, and the money from soldiering added fuel to the fire that was burning me up from the inside out. I was miserable, although most people would never know it. My family did, though, and they let me know from time to time how they felt.

My time in the Middle East included some amazing adventures. For a while I was stationed about twenty miles from Tyre, an ancient Phoenician port city and one of the oldest continuously inhabited cities in the world. Tyre was also the last stop on the Mediterranean for the Silk Road, the lucrative trade route that connected the East and the West. Part of the actual road is still used between Tyre and Damascus today.

I was fascinated by the road to Damascus because I remembered learning about it in school—how the apostle Paul, who was also known as Saul, had been a stone-cold killer of the people who followed Jesus. He was on the road to Damascus when a bright light from heaven literally stopped him in his tracks. Saul was blinded, and Jesus appeared to him right there, called him out, and changed the course of his life. Three days later, he had his eyesight back, and even more important, he had a new vision for his life—to tell people about Jesus. One encounter on the road to Damascus completely rerouted him.

A couple of times I drove down that same road Paul had traveled and wondered what it would have been like to see that bright light, but I wasn't ready for that much illumination just yet. I was still too strong, too independent, too proud. Or maybe I was too afraid to do something different.

I did break down and say the odd prayer or two, asking God for protection whenever I got into a bad situation. One night while I was still on active duty in Lebanon, I was out with a friend named Connor. He was a brilliant soccer player and a funny little guy who put up with a lot from me. I was always jumping on him and wrestling him to the ground for fun.

We had driven into Beirut to watch an important soccer game and were on our way home. When we left the base to head to the game, we were dressed in civilian clothes. We had to leave our rifles, ammo, and flak jackets behind. This protocol was established to help us mix in with the locals and avoid any confrontations that could quickly escalate in such a volatile atmosphere.

When we got to the pub after the game, I quickly made myself merry, but Connor was in a sour mood because his team had lost. When it was over, we hopped back into the Jeep with me at the wheel, and we headed toward the hills on the road back to Sidon.

We were driving, minding our own business, when I got confused on a turn, slowed down to figure it out, and BAM! Something hit us from behind.

We both looked around and had no idea what just happened. I took a deep breath. *This isn't good.* The last thing you want to do in a place where it's hard to tell the good guys from the bad is to get into a public traffic altercation.

Then *BAM!* It hit us again.

Now we could see it. A beat-up white Mercedes roared up to the side of us, full of Hezbollah guerrilla fighters in full jihad mode. We were the enemy here, and we were unarmed. This wasn't looking good at all.

They pulled an AK-47 out of the back seat and stuck it out the window, pointed right at us. Needless to say, I slammed the Jeep into gear and took off down the road toward Sidon while Connor fired up the radio and started yelling out frantic requests for the gatekeeper at the UN post to open the gate for us.

It was a high-speed chase for miles, bumper to bumper, me using every shred of Irish driving skill I had learned on the bumpy lanes of County Cork to stay ahead of the death-wagon Mercedes on our tail.

"Connor, we're dead here," I kept shouting. "We're actually dead."

Connor kept on the radio, and thanks be to God the gates were wide open when we arrived. We flew through, and when the Mercedes tried to follow, the guns came out and there was a big standoff. We were safe, at least for the moment.

The military police met us as we stopped the car and got out. We were now part of an international incident, and even though we were delighted to be alive and not lying on the side of the road full of bullet holes, the MPs had an investigation to do.

We had one big worry—we reeked of alcohol.

They put us in a room to wait. We were distraught. What was going to happen?

We knew they were going to question us. "We have to do something!" Connor said, looking like he was about to panic.

I got up to look out the window. "We're either going to be sent away and locked up in a UN cell somewhere or get a quick trip home." I turned and saw a door in the wall and decided to try it. Behind the door was a food prep area, with a big bowl of onions sitting on the counter. That sparked an idea for something I'd learned at a young age.

I grabbed two onions. "Connor, quick. Catch this!" I tossed one to Connor as I took a bite of mine. We chomped and chewed as if our lives depended on it, which they did. I was hoping the onions would overpower the smell of alcohol on our breath. It had worked for Barry, Brendan, Sean, Bryan, and me time and again when we were adolescents and needed to keep our parents from finding out that we had been drinking. But I'd forgotten about the other effect onions could have on you. Connor and I both started crying like babies, tears running down our cheeks. Once we started, we couldn't stop.

Just then an MP burst into the room, took one look at Connor, and said loudly with an African accent, "Okay, what is the story? What is wrong with this man?"

We were both still in shock and didn't say anything as the tears continued to flow down Connor's face, dripping off his chin.

"It's okay, you stupid man," the MP said. "There's no need to cry! It's okay. There is nobody dead!"

He turned around and fled the room. I guess he wasn't able to deal with Connor's crying and was relieved to hand us off to someone who put us in another room for the night. The situation was resolved behind the scenes the next day. The front of the Mercedes was badly damaged and they blamed us for it—but it had been a serious situation. The onions were the only funny part about it; we were lucky to escape with our lives.

After that, Connor told everyone I was a jinx and advised them to avoid going on patrol with me. It was hard to tell if we actually got shot at by Hezbollah, what with the banging of cars and clouds of dust everywhere, but if they had fired the AK-47 and hit us, the end of the story would have been very different.

Another night I was driving a tank on patrol when we encountered a group of Hezbollah in a pickup truck at about three in the morning. We were on a dark road, and their pickup had a mortar bolted to the bed of the truck—much more maneuverable than our tank. I couldn't go forward or backward because I was hemmed in by the pickup in front of me, a UN personnel carrier behind me, dusty houses on one side, and a sheer drop-off into a massive canyon on the other.

Eventually Hezbollah gave up, realizing they were outgunned, but that and the onion incident reminded me there was a God and I needed to be on a first-name basis with him. He had listened to my quick prayers of desperation and gotten me out of those two situations, as well as many more. But I just wasn't ready to change. I was going to need a road-to-Damascus moment like Paul.

While the danger of serving in the military was real, my time in the Middle East and later in Kosovo introduced me to new people and new parts of the world. I met people from France, Spain, Norway, Fiji, Poland, Africa, India, and Nepal. Lebanon was the biggest UN deployment location in the world at the time, bringing in people from all over the world to help keep the peace. The sky in Lebanon was beautiful with blankets of stars stretching across the deep black sky, and gazing up at it gave me a little bit of peace, similar to what I had experienced many times on the rock at the sanctuary. On patrol breaks, I'd lie on top of the tank under the sky and think about Mam and Dad, my sisters and friends, the village, and the people I loved who had gone before me, all their faces flashing in front of my eyes. I sipped coffee from my flask and felt an emptiness deep inside. I knew my family loved me, but I still wanted someone for my very own, someone to complete me.

Maybe my *anam cara* was looking up at those same stars, somewhere else in the world, waiting for me. Maybe the promised land was out there somewhere for me, and I could find my place and my people and finally feel like I belonged.

ꙩbe ꙩan
in ꙩbe ꙍinꙨoꙍ

My past, O Lord, to Your mercy;
my present, to Your love;
my future to Your providence.

PADRE PIO

A DONKEY ONCE CAME INTO THE SANCTUARY with a very unique addiction. His owner was an older woman who couldn't care for him anymore, so she called us and we were happy to take the donkey. As we were loading him into the horse box for the journey back to Liscarroll, she handed us a big box.

"You need to give him two of these every day," she insisted loudly. Inside the box were two hundred Mars Bars.

I can report that the majority of the candy bars made it back to the sanctuary, and the rescued donkey with the sweet tooth got his two candy bars a day . . . for a while. Of course, sweets loaded with chocolate and sugar aren't good for donkeys and are not part of their typical diet, but because it had become a daily habit, he had to be weaned off of them slowly.

Everyone working at the donkey sanctuary was more than

happy to help dispose of the candy bars by having one with after-noon tea, and by the time the box was empty, Mars (the donkey's new name) was officially on his way to normal donkey fare. He probably wondered what had happened to his treats, but he was okay.

Not long after his rehabilitation period, the older lady showed up at the donkey sanctuary one day bearing a special gift—a fresh box of candy bars for her furry friend! This time around, we grate-fully accepted her donation, and all of us enjoyed them, with the exception of Mars. I like to think that Mars donated his sweets to the humans who were helping him.

A typical healthy donkey diet is what we call "haylage," a mix-ture of hay and silage. Hay is dried grasses with grain heads from the fields, and silage is chopped up grasses that are fermented, dried, and then kept in a silo. They typically do well eating some straw, such as barley straw, with a coating of haylage on the top; this provides them with all the different nutrients they need in the winter. In summer, a bit of grazing is good and something they enjoy, but donkeys need strict limits so they don't overdo it.

Donkeys don't do well on a steady, all-you-can-eat diet of sweet fresh grass. They tend to gorge themselves and can end up with all sorts of health issues, including laminitis, a very painful (and serious) inflammation of the feet. The way to keep donkeys from eating too much fresh grass is simple—put up a fence. You either permanently fence off the pastures into smaller sections and rotate the donkeys around or use a portable fence to do the same thing. In either case, you limit the amount of time a donkey is on grass and stop them when they've had enough. It's easier said than done, though. Donkeys like to open gates (remember Aran?) or get down on their knees and sneak under fences. Although the joy on a don-key's face when you open a gate and let them into a fresh pasture is beautiful, too much grass can kill them.

I wish someone could have put a portable fence around me to keep me from overindulging in what was bad for me because I couldn't seem to stop on my own. When I walked into a pub, I felt like a donkey released in a fresh green pasture, but for me it was no field of dreams. By the time I was in my mid-twenties, and ready to get out of the army, I'd been drinking for almost twenty years.

Unlike the donkeys, I wasn't putting on weight when I overindulged; I was getting thinner. My alcohol consumption level was so high I didn't have much of an appetite. I only ate food so I could drink.

Mars really did not have a choice on whether to continue his addiction or not—that choice was taken out of his hands when he arrived at the sanctuary. But that was not my reality because I *did* have a choice of whether to get help, and I wouldn't ask for it.

I ended up serving five years total in Lebanon and Kosovo with the Irish Defence Forces, participating in two peacekeeping missions and one peace enforcer mission. Though I was tasked with keeping the peace on an international level, I had no peace of my own. Life was dark for me, and I still didn't have a sense of purpose. I was adrift in every way, and I'd lost most of the safe bonds to home and those who loved me.

When I got out of the army, I let my hair grow long, my cheekbones were sunken in, and my mental and emotional state showed in my eyes. My mind, heart, and spirit were sick. I didn't know it yet, but I was suffering from PTSD.

I had never fully recovered from Anita's untimely death, the Valentine's Day accident near Beirut, and the other traumatic experiences that make up the life of a soldier in a war zone populated by terrorists. One small memory that still upsets me is the story of some locals, I'm not sure on what side, who devised a donkey bomb by packing a donkey carcass with explosives and leaving it by the side of the road to be triggered by a remote. This wasn't the worst of what I saw and heard, but it was brutal and unforgettable.

No one is quite sure why some people experience PTSD while others do not, and further, why some people who suffer PTSD recover quickly, while others suffer for years, or even a lifetime. More is known about the condition now, but when I was leaving the army, nothing much was said about it. I was offered medication that I refused, and there weren't other options available for someone like me.

Now that I was a civilian, I couldn't seem to shift out of the war zone mindset. I was stuck in a permanent state of fight-or-flight, with anxiety, anger, depression, nightmares, and paranoia I couldn't shake. In the army I had tested and proven my strength and endurance, but in the real world, the shadows inside me were growing.

My five years in the military started me on a descent into deep darkness, and by the time I got out I was suicidal, although I told no one, not even my family. The only things that took the edge off my pain and numbed me were alcohol and illegal drugs. But even those substances didn't work for long.

I went back to Liscarroll to visit my family, although I didn't plan on staying. I wanted to try my fortunes in London, like my great-grandfather had done when he worked for Scotland Yard. But for now, while I was at home, it was business as usual, with hours spent in pubs in all the different villages.

One day I was at a nightclub in Mallow and came out of the front door just as a guard approached. I stumbled and fell down in front of the club, and the guard bent down to pick me up. I had no idea what he intended to do, and I immediately went into a full-blown panic, thinking someone was after me. My body was steeped in alcohol and drugs, and something snapped inside of me. I elbowed him in the chin as hard as I could, then took off running at full speed down the street. His partner saw what happened and started after me in the patrol car, eventually blocking me, but I jumped up on the car, rolled off the hood, and kept running.

I ran around the block, headed to the famous village Clock House, ran for a mile or two beyond, then doubled back through a wooded area to throw off any pursuers. In my mind, I was a fox and I had to get away from the hunter. *Evade and escape.*

On my way back into town, I ran through a construction area, and when I came to a twelve-foot-high chain link fence, I just ran right up it, grabbing a handhold here and there, until I could almost reach the top. It was insane, but I was still very strong from the army, and I was fueled by adrenaline and the need to get away. The guards had caught up with me, and one grabbed my foot and dragged me back down.

I went berserk, tackling officers and using military pressure holds. It took five men to subdue me. They hauled me off to jail and made it very clear by how they treated me that they were unhappy with my behavior. I blacked out and woke up in the hospital. I wasn't clear about what had happened; the memory was an out-of-focus film. As he had done so many times before, Dad helped me deal with the legal consequences.

Another day I was on an all-day drinking binge after a Gaelic football match, and I felt ravenous—but not for food. I wanted more and more drink. I couldn't seem to get enough. I'm sure my blood was mostly alcohol by the time my friends decided to abandon me because they were scared of my driving. I tried to talk them out of it, but they refused to get back in the car.

"Brilliant!" I shouted in disappointment, jamming my white Ford Mondeo into gear and screeching away. I was proud of the new car I had bought with my army money, and I liked to drive fast. I zoomed off to go dancing at another club, had a few more drinks, then headed back to Liscarroll.

It was late, and somewhere near Lisgriffin I came around a corner and, in the glare of my headlights, saw several huge black bulls standing in the middle of the road.

I can't get around them! my mind screamed. I have no idea how fast I was going but it was too fast to stop. At the last second, I slammed on the brakes, jerked my steering wheel to the right, and *BAM!* crashed at high speed into a solid stone wall.

The sudden impact knocked me out. I never saw or felt the stones from the wall toppling over, crushing the roof of my car and crashing through the windscreen. I must have been unconscious for a while because when I woke up in the darkness, I couldn't get my bearings. *What's going on? Where am I?* I knew I needed help—I didn't know what my injuries were like or if I could even get out of the car.

Then I heard footsteps. Was someone there?

"Help," I cried out. My voice came out weak so I tried harder. "Help me. Is someone there? I need help."

Footsteps again. This time I listened and heard what sounded like steps circling my car. They were quiet and deliberate, but I couldn't hear anything else beyond the crunch of the steps.

"Help!" I called out again and again, but the footsteps stopped, and I never heard them again.

The relief of hearing the steps cleared my head a bit, and I began to realize what had happened. I tried shifting myself a bit and found that I could move. I pushed aside some rocks, wrestled with the smashed-up door, and climbed out of the car. I checked my arms and legs and was relieved to find that I could move everything. I didn't seem to be badly injured. I pulled out my cell phone and called my brother-in-law, Tim. When he arrived, I reached into the wrecked car, pulled out my keys, and locked the doors.

"What happened here?" Tim looked at me with a frown.

"There were some black bullocks in the road."

"Hmm." He looked skeptical.

I rubbed my head and eyes, starting to feel sore from the roof caving in on top of me. "When I woke up I heard some footsteps, but whoever it was went away."

I didn't think much about what Tim must have thought about me at that moment. All I wanted to do was get home, collapse on the sofa, and sleep for the rest of the day.

When Tim dropped me off, I stumbled inside Mam and Dad's house. The last thing I remember was hearing Dad on the phone, calling the tow truck company and arranging for them to pick up my car. We'd have to deal with the wall too. Damaging a stone wall in Ireland is taken seriously, and repairs are not cheap. At least I had the money.

Hours later, I heard Dad calling my name. "Patrick. I want to show you what I found in your car." He held out his hand and opened his fingers, palm up.

It was a Padre Pio medal, with a picture of the popular twentieth-century bearded saint from Italy.

What? Why are you showing me a religious medal? It made no sense.

"I found this on the dashboard of your car. It was balanced right on the edge of the dashboard, behind your steering wheel, hanging half off." His eyes were wide.

"It's not mine. I don't have one." I was still half asleep and not really comprehending what he was saying.

Later, when I had sobered up a bit, Dad told me that while he was standing next to my car, waiting for the tow truck to arrive, he'd used my key to open the driver's side door and look inside at the damage.

"I couldn't believe you didn't get hurt," he said. "And then I saw the medal."

Dad's favorite Catholic saint was Padre Pio, an Italian priest known to be a man of prayer and of suffering, and Dad was comforted when he found the medal. He believed that Padre Pio himself had walked around my car and helped me. In the end, we never figured out how the medal came to be in my car, balanced on the dashboard, or what the footsteps were, or where the black bulls went (if they were even there). It was all a mystery, one of many in Ireland.

My parents continued to pray for me over those dark years, and I believe it's because of them that I survived. I know someone was watching over me and keeping me alive. I was still a lost and broken man, a wild donkey who had strayed far from his herd and needed help. But I wasn't ready to accept it, not yet.

Not long after, I was in the city of London working odd jobs. I lived in a flat with a new girlfriend, and when she got pregnant I hoped starting a family might help me settle down. Maybe having a family to support and children to live for would solve my problems and bring me some peace and happiness.

But the reality didn't match up with my dreams. My girlfriend and I started arguing about everything, and I would go into uncontrollable rages, as if a red mist enveloped my brain and clouded my thinking. I was binge drinking at the pubs regularly, and when I came out, I'd sometimes sleep at the train station or on a park bench near a pond where I could listen to the ducks and geese. Other nights, when my paranoia got out of control, I'd end up in the hospital emergency ward, being wrestled down by a big male nurse. I kept screaming that I was being watched and that helicopters were following me.

One night I started banging my head on a French door in the flat and ended up putting my head through a pane of glass. Other times, when I was alone and descending into a kind of dark dream world, I started cutting my wrist with a serrated knife, going deeper and deeper, just trying to feel something and make sure I was alive. I was like a raw and temperamental hand grenade that could go off at any time.

I hated myself and the man I'd become. Or maybe I wasn't a man at all, but rather some kind of dark monster. The darkness inside of me felt like it had taken over, morphing into a sort of shadow man who was running my life and calling the shots. I had no vision for a future, and now with a baby coming, I wondered what kind of life this was going to be for a child.

My parents tried to call, but I avoided them, though sometimes I ran out of money and had to call them for a loan. My sisters tried to talk to me many times.

"What's going on with you?" Helen or Debbie would ask. "Things aren't right!"

"Leave me alone. I'm grand." I didn't want anyone to be annoying me.

Leave me alone to drink.

I was scared of ending up like Mam's brother Noel, a schizophrenic who lived and died on the streets of London. He was a creative and gifted photographer, and my mam really loved him, but the love of his family wasn't enough to save him. I wondered if he'd been ashamed like me and didn't want anyone to know what he was going through.

One particularly bad night I was walking down High Street in the London borough of Richmond. My girlfriend and I had had another big fight, and after that I'd gone to a pub and discovered my hometown Munster rugby team had never even reached the finals. My anger flared as I walked down the street, darkness and despair settling down on me like a black Irish storm blowing down across the landscape.

I stopped and looked at my reflection in a big plate glass window. The eyes in the window were black like the darkest shadows. *Who are you?* I thought. *What is wrong with you! Why can't you get your life straight? Why can't you get it together!*

I didn't feel like flesh and blood and spirit anymore. All I saw in the window was darkness, a man made of shadow that blotted out the light.

I wanted to shout and cry, but I knew if I started, I'd never stop. I couldn't stand to look at myself anymore, so I made a fist and punched my hand straight through the glass.

The window cracked on impact and broke apart, glass raining down inside and out.

I walked away, too intoxicated to feel anything and not even realizing I had a piece of glass the size of a large dagger sticking out of the underside of my forearm. A moment later, my skin prickled a bit, and without thinking, I reached over and pulled the shard out of my arm.

I walked about six feet before blood began spurting from my arm, and I fell onto the footpath. As I crumpled to the ground, everything became dark, and I felt like I was falling backward, down into a lightless tunnel.

I remember looking up, and that's when I saw a blonde woman. *What's Mam doing here? How did she find me?*

I was so glad she was there, holding my hand and pressing against the gash on my arm to slow the bleeding.

I began to come around a bit, and I saw my mam more clearly. Somehow she'd flown across the Irish Sea and found me! She knew I needed help, and she was right there with me.

"Mam, please don't leave me," I cried out. I was getting weaker as I lost more blood, but the excruciating pain in my arm kept me semi-conscious. I still didn't know what had happened. I thought it was the drink. I didn't understand why I was so weak, because I was usually able to handle my alcohol.

"I'm here," Mam said. "I'm here. You're going to be okay." She was kneeling on my arm now, applying pressure with her knee, and holding my hand in hers. I wasn't scared, because Mam was there.

I can always count on you, Mam.

I woke up in a bed in London's Kingston Hospital, groggy and confused. My arm was wrapped in bandages like a mummy and propped up on several pillows. *What happened? Why am I here?*

The nurse and surgeon filled me in. The glass shard had sliced my artery and nearly severed a tendon, and when I was brought in, I was down to my last liter and a half of blood. Emergency surgery had not only saved my arm—it had saved my life.

The incident had happened in front of an Indian restaurant. The blonde woman I thought was Mam was a server who had run outside with a towel, wrapped it around my arm, and kept pressure on the wound until the paramedics arrived. She insisted on riding in the ambulance with me, waited through my surgery, and stayed with me in the hospital room a good part of the night while I slept.

The stranger was my angel, and she saved my life. I never saw her again, and I still don't know who she is.

CHAPTER TEN

ᏋᎪᏋ ᎪᏁᎠ ᎠᎪᎠ

Two shorten the road.

IRISH PROVERB

IRISH WOMEN ARE STRONG, like steel cloaked in silk, and Mam is the strongest of them all. She kept our house running and our family together while my dad was out picking up donkeys and bringing them home for her to care for—another mouth to feed, another life to protect, and she took it all in stride. My mam always made me feel safe, and I knew she would always be there for me.

I once heard a story from America about a jenny who fought off a mountain lion that was attacking the family goat. The owner woke up in the middle of the night to terrible screeching, ran outside, and saw a mountain lion gripping the goat's face in its teeth. The man began yelling at the lion, but it did nothing. Then his pet donkey approached the lion, braying at the top of her lungs. She put her ears back, bared her teeth, and began lunging and biting at the hindquarters of the mountain lion, braying all the while.

At that point the lion could have let the goat go, turned around and attacked the donkey, but it knew better. Instead, it released the goat and took off, never to be seen again. Smart lion!

Wild donkey herds are matriarchal, led by a strong jenny who keeps a close eye on the herd and maintains order. She keeps her female offspring with her for life, but she drives the jacks off when they get old enough to breed. The jacks go off and form their own bachelor herd but are allowed to come back to breed.

At the donkey sanctuary the herds are managed, not wild, but you can still see that the jenny decides where the herd grazes, when to take refuge in the barn during bad weather, and when to go in for hay. She also keeps order, using her body language to keep the peace between the other donkeys and to reward or punish those who need it.

Once we had a jenny in season named Nutmeg. She was a real rip—strong and feisty. One night a gelding broke into her paddock and wouldn't leave her alone. Nutmeg wasn't in the mood to be harassed, so she turned around and kicked him with her two hind feet right upside his head, square on the jaw, and knocked him to the ground. The poor chap was out cold.

A donkey can cross a line and turn vicious—there have been cases where a donkey has actually killed a person, and they routinely attack and kill dogs who invade their territory. So teaching a donkey good manners is crucial for human safety and welfare.

The lead jenny also rounds up stragglers and wanderers. Often a younger donkey, or maybe just a clueless or stubborn one, will get separated from the herd and be off grazing by himself in a clump of bushes. Because the youngster is not paying attention, he misses the cues to get with the group, move to another location, and head back to the barn at night. But the boss lady misses nothing and will circle back, get his attention with a nip of her teeth and a shove of her muscled shoulder, and lead him back to safety.

My mam was the matriarch of our herd, and she was my rock—strong, protective, loyal, and caring. Her life wasn't easy, and she had grown strong and resilient enough to carry all of our problems along with her own. Mam sacrificed so much of her life for our family and for me, and I've heard people say that the donkey sanctuary wouldn't have happened without her and the fierce, hard work she put in.

She is an introvert and a deep thinker who doesn't say much, but she shows her feelings by taking care of others. Dad is an extrovert who loves people and is a great communicator. You could say Dad was the face and Mam was the backbone of the sanctuary.

One of the only times I ever saw her cry is when she broke her wrist. She tried to carry two heavy buckets of water, but it was impossible. Mam sat in her room and cried, "I can't do anything!"

But, of course, she could. She could be there like she always was, and she could love us like she always did. But it wasn't enough for her. She wanted to be useful.

Mam was born Eileen MacCormack into a family of thirteen children in the small village of Littleton in County Tipperary. She was the oldest of three girls, with ten brothers, some older and some younger, putting Mam right in the middle. Her mam, my nana, struggled with some health problems, so Mam reared the younger half of the family herself. That meant hard physical labor—cooking, washing, feeding and changing the babies while minding the older children at the same time.

Nana had been adopted, the circumstances similar to my sister Eileen's situation, and she was raised by her biological aunt and uncle. No one knew who my great-grandfather was, and Nana was blessed that her family of origin took her in, as unwed pregnant girls during that time were often sent to "institutes" run by the church. These mothers and their illegitimate children were sometimes subject to abuse and mistreatment.

Mam's dad was a locomotive driver who worked for the sugar beet factory in nearby Thurles. He worked hard, putting in twelve- to fourteen-hour shifts, and came home exhausted. To help him relax, my mom's younger, red-headed sister, Mary, played the fiddle. She is a gifted musician who can play any instrument she puts her hands on. Mary had a hard time in school and later found out she was dyslexic. I know how she felt!

When Mam was young, one of her little brothers, baby Philip, died of scarlet fever. She still has a vivid memory of his little white coffin. Mam had scarlet fever too, but a neighbor boiled up some arrowroot, which was thought to bring down a high temperature, and Mam recovered after a couple of weeks.

The family lived in a small cottage on an acre of land with a big vegetable garden full of potatoes, turnips, cabbage, lettuce, parsnips, and beets. Her dad made enough to feed the family, but there was no extra, and Mam had to quit school at twelve because she couldn't afford to pay for her books.

A large fireplace kept the stone floor in the cottage warm and this was where all the cooking was done. Her mother would hang a pot of Irish stew on a metal arm called a crane, and as it bubbled over the fire, it filled the room with a mouthwatering aroma. The pope looked down from the wall where his picture was proudly displayed, while the kids ran their toothbrushes along the inside of the chimney, and then brushed their teeth with the black soot. My uncles had nice white teeth, so it must have worked.

"You have to mind your teeth," Mam always told me. "You have no excuse—you have running water!"

The babies slept in an actual chest of drawers, with the smaller babies in the upper drawers and the bigger babies toward the bottom. The cottage had no electricity or running water. Kerosene lanterns offered some light, and water had to be fetched from a pump down the road. Mam and her siblings carried buckets of water back to the cottage every day for drinking, cooking, laundry, and filling the big tin bathtub in front of the fire. In the summer, the family bathed in the river Breagagh.

When she was seven or eight years old, Mam and her siblings helped her dad cut sod from the local peat bog to dry and use for fuel in the fireplace. Picture a child standing in a damp, muddy field, sometimes in cold standing water, and helping cut heavy, soggy wet bricks out of the earth with a two-sided spade called a *sleán*. Next, the bricks were lifted out of the bog, piled carefully into stacks of a dozen or more, left to dry, and then later rotated to dry some more.

The children weren't supposed to miss school, but their dad needed them. So on the way to the bog fields, they all hid under a blanket in the donkey cart as it rolled past the school, the headmaster none the wiser. No one was sorry to miss school. The teachers and the headmaster were strict and severe, and if you answered a question incorrectly, you got a beating, or worse.

It was a long journey from Littleton to the bog in Langool— about fifteen miles—and it was backbreaking work when they finally arrived. People cutting sod often used donkey carts to transport what they harvested, intentionally letting the animal's hooves grow long and curved, almost like skis. The result was painful for the donkeys, but it kept them from sinking down into the wetland muck.

But life wasn't all work. Mam and her siblings played hopscotch, tag, and marbles, blew bubbles out of the laundry water, and pitched horseshoes at the crossroads. The girls even did a bit of hurling with their brothers on the local pitch. Mam could hit a good ball. They had a dog named Rex and a donkey named Grayback, whom they loved.

Mam and the rest of the kids learned to step dance at Miss Wiggins School of Dancing. Mam was an especially brilliant dancer and won some awards. She and Mary were proud of their dance costumes: a green jacket with a Tara brooch on a cream sash across her chest, and a cream pleated skirt with rich embroidery on the front.

When Mam was fourteen, she was recruited to be a chambermaid for two wealthy brothers at a big house in London called The Grove, a stately two-story Georgian mansion of red brick. It was similar work to what she was already used to—cooking, washing, and cleaning—but in a nicer setting with running water, and with much higher standards. The work hours were long with little freedom and only one evening off every few weeks. It was slavery, really, and Mam lost her childhood. Most of the money she made was sent back to her family in Ireland.

Going into service wasn't as glamorous and interesting as the movies and television programs might make it seem. It was grueling work, and the sleeping quarters were either in a cold drafty attic or a basement room. Servants weren't allowed to talk to the family members they served without permission, they had to "give room" if they accidentally met a family member or guest on the stairs or in a hallway and avert their gaze.

Irish maids were in demand in Britain because they were plentiful and could be paid a much lower salary, but they were considered inferior to Scottish and English servants. Irish servants and other workers were seen as slow, stupid, and uneducated.

Because of this imbalance of power, chambermaids were sometimes treated poorly and taken advantage of in many ways. Picture a fourteen-year-old girl from a small rural village in Ireland, who had a roof over her head and warm food (usually leftovers) to eat in nice surroundings, but at the same time was suddenly alone and far from home, with no one to protect her and keep her safe other than the other servants—if they were kind. It was survival of the fittest. Mam grew stronger and tougher, and she survived.

Mary joined Mam at The Grove a few years later when she turned fourteen. Mary was considered wild compared to her quiet older sister, but the two sisters were very close and watched out for each other on this new adventure. At the train station in Thurles, Mary remembers that her dad shook her hand to say goodbye as she left for Dublin, then a ferry to England—no hugs, kisses, or I love yous.

Each year for three months during hunting season, the servant staff went with the family to Glenborough Lodge in Perthshire, their lodge in the Scottish Highlands. There was plenty of wild game to eat—grouse, pheasant, goose, partridge, and hare.

Occasionally, Mary and Mam were given a few hours off to ride the family horses, two big black Shires named Moses and Fly. The two girls, one with golden hair and one with fiery red, loved these rare moments. They would pack a lunch and ride out on the horses to explore forests, glens, and rivers, before stopping to picnic at a glorious waterfall. It could have—should have—been idyllic. But the reality is Mary lost her childhood too.

Dad was born in the two-story rock house in Liscarroll, the house where my grandmother gave me that first glass of sherry. At that time, the rock house was located on a thirty-five-acre dairy farm with fifty-five Friesian cows.

My great-grandfather, Patrick (Paddy) Bresnihan, was originally from Limerick. Paddy was a smart man who taught himself how to read and write, and when he was old enough, he took the exams for the Metropolitan Police in London, also known as Scotland Yard. He purchased the farm in Liscarroll to move to when he retired as a chief inspector. He bred and trained champion

Scottish Highland Terriers, a moneymaking enterprise that he enjoyed, and he wanted more room to raise the dogs. At the time the farm covered more than a hundred acres, and it included an old lime kiln, the fields and the stream, the hill with the rock, the ruined watchtower, and the ring fort that looked down on the castle.

Paddy was a memorable character in the village and didn't go to church except on Christmas Day, when he marched up the aisle and sat in the front pew.

He arranged for the rock house to be built with stones from the ruins of Ballybeg Monastery, long ago destroyed by the Vikings, and when he died on Palm Sunday in 1945, he was buried in Knawhill Cemetery. You can see his dream house from his grave. I inherited his desk, a retirement gift that is now more than a hundred years old.

Back in my great-grandfather's day, Liscarroll was a thriving village with a couple of thousand inhabitants who filled the townhouses along the main street, many with businesses on the ground floor, as well as the surrounding estates and farms. In the village's heyday, there were creameries and dairy farmers, builders and thatchers, butchers, ironmongers, coalmen, council workers, gardeners and farm workers, postmasters and postal workers, blacksmiths, schoolteachers, undertakers, newsagents (who sold newspapers), lorry drivers, shopkeepers, barbers, hackney drivers, mechanics, confectioners, guards, priests, and publicans.

Paddy and his wife, Julia, who was from Liscarroll, had a daughter named Eileen, who married Garrett Barrett from Mallow (the same town where I ran out of the pub and led the police on the miles-long chase). Eileen and Garrett inherited the rock house when my great-grandparents died, and they had five children, including my father, Paddy.

My grandfather Garrett was an animal welfare inspector for the

Irish Society for the Prevention of Cruelty to Animals (ISPCA), and my grandmother Eileen helped run the dairy farm. There were donkeys there in the fields starting back in 1926, and my grand-dad had a vision for the farm to become a place for animals who needed a safe haven.

My granddad was quiet and unassuming; he never laid a hand on his children, rare in Ireland at that time. Granddad was also very religious. Dad remembers seeing him on his hands and knees praying. I have granddad's Rosary beads. I also have his St. Jude medal that he found on the floor of the hay barn. Dad gave it to me during final exams for high school. It's old and worn and a treasure. I carried it in my wallet when I was in the army and when I lived in London. One night I couldn't find it and was sure I lost it at a nightclub. For weeks I looked for it and finally gave up. Then, one night it was there, right on my dresser, a treasure found again. Ironically, St. Jude is the patron saint of lost causes, and I still carry his medal.

Dad, a redhead with green eyes, had a lot of energy as a boy and loved spending time with the animals, including a pet donkey named Neddy and his dog Buddy, who followed him everywhere, especially to the rock. Dad loved it up there as much as I did. His school experience was like mine—he suffered countless beatings. His younger brother Brendan was due to inherit the farm, so Dad was sent away to boarding school at twelve to become a priest, a great honor to an Irish family.

There were ten priests staffing the boarding school; eight of them were warm, friendly, wise teachers, and two of them were bullies. One brutal man would beat Dad down to the ground, viciously kick him once he had fallen, and give him another kick for good measure.

Dad didn't dare tell his family about the beatings or ask to go home for fear of even worse treatment from the priests. He still carries the emotional scars of those beatings. I've heard him wake up screaming from nightmares. But it also gave him incredible empathy for donkeys that have been abused.

Dad was crushed by this treatment and felt like he was in prison. He wanted to be a farmer, but he had no land. So when he was eighteen, he left the rock house and the green hills and vales of Liscarroll and emigrated to London to go to college and find work.

One evening in London, both my parents were at an Irish dance hall called Gresham Ballroom. The luckiest thing in the world happened to Dad when he saw Mam and walked over to her. My beautiful blonde mam, the award-winning Irish step dancer, put out her hand. Dad took it and they danced the night away. Before the evening was over, he asked for her phone number and got it.

A few weeks later, Dad became deathly ill with the flu.

His landlady started to worry. "Do ye have any family?" she asked.

"I have a friend," Dad said. "Her number is in the pocket of my coat." The landlady found the slip of paper with Mam's number, called her, and three hours later Mam knocked on the door of Dad's one-bedroom flat, bringing a homemade pot of soup and a bottle of whiskey. For Dad, it was love at second sight when Mam came in, her blue eyes sparkling, carrying a little taste of Irish hospitality for a young man far from home.

⊷⟩═◉ ◉═⟨⊶

Mam and Dad married in London at Edmonton Church with a handful of guests. Mam's brother Eddy was there, and so was Dad's brother Gary, and his wife, Emily. Unfortunately, Mary wasn't permitted to take a day off work to come to her own sister's wedding.

A few years later, Mam and Dad ended up back in Liscarroll with four small children to live in a small house next door to the rock house, where my grandparents still lived. I was one year old.

Dad sometimes helped his father at the ISPCA in the 1980s. Some of the Irish viewed their animals, including donkeys, more like machines to be used and abused than living animals to be treated humanely. It was not easy work for someone with a sensitive, caring heart like Dad. I remember many times Dad would come home in tears after a heart-wrenching rescue or when a donkey was beyond hope and had to be put down.

Donkeys originally came from Northern Africa, the Middle East, India, and Tibet, where they ran wild in herds. Some of these wild donkeys still exist, but they are critically endangered. Donkeys are cousins to zebras and horses, in the *Equus* family tree. Donkeys, or *asal* in Irish, were brought to Ireland in the 1100s, about the same time Liscarroll Castle was built. Legions of sure-footed donkeys served as work animals on farms all over the country, pulling heavy carts full of sod, vegetables, or rocks and carrying baskets or even people on their backs. In 1914, an estimated 256,000 donkeys lived in Ireland.

Later, the donkey became a symbol of what some people loved about the island—a quaint world of rural beauty and charm, full of thatched-roof cottages, happy children, and old women tending their spinning wheels with an adorable donkey in the background. The reality was that parts of Ireland were impoverished, due to a complicated history that included colonization, religious oppression, and famine. But even when tractors became more prevalent, plenty of people still wanted a donkey as a pet without a clue on how much work it takes to properly care for them.

We had lived in Liscarroll for just a year when Dad was out on an ISPCA call with his father. They were investigating a farmer who had cruelly hobbled his cattle with ropes. My grandfather was outraged and walked through the field with a big knife, cutting the bindings off the cattle to set them free.

Suddenly, grandfather's left arm began to shake, and he handed the knife to my dad. "Will you do it, Paddy?"

Dad took the knife and then looked at grandfather's face, now pale.

"Are you okay?" he asked his father.

"I'm all right, I'm all right," said my grandfather. But he wasn't. Within moments, grandfather dropped to the ground, dead from a heart attack at the age of sixty. There was nothing Dad could do.

Dad was still in shock when he came home and told us what happened. I was two years old, so I don't remember much at all, but my sister Helen was devastated and cried, "My best granddad is dead!"

Dad ended up inheriting the farm in Liscarroll from Nana. (His brother inherited a different farm in Killavullen.) At the age of thirty-four, Dad felt like his father's mantle and vision for an animal sanctuary had fallen onto him. Dad began in earnest to rescue donkeys that needed a home and bring them back to our farm to be doctored and cared for. He started off by putting the donkeys in small barns and sheds around the property. At first it was known as the Richard Martin Rescue Field, after an Irish politician in the 1700s who campaigned against mistreatment of animals. Martin was a champion dueler known as "Hairtrigger Dick," who originated the RSPCA and became known as the savior of animals in Ireland.

Later Dad founded his own charity organization, called The Donkey Sanctuary of Ireland, to support the work. He handed out pamphlets at fairs and horse shows, did talks at schools and agricultural events, and started a newsletter to get the word out.

In 1987, Dad joined forces with Dr. Elisabeth Svendsen at the Donkey Sanctuary in England.

Eventually, people who donated money to the Donkey Sanctuary wanted to visit, to see where their money was going. Dad decided to waive the admission fee and encouraged visitors to make donations or adopt a donkey. Word got out, and people came to meet the donkeys and tour the sanctuary. Dad loved educating the public on how to care for donkeys and keep them healthy and safe. His first concern was the welfare of the donkey. All of us helped out as children, and most of us worked there as adults at one time or another. It was a family mission.

The donkeys at the sanctuary were often half wild, afraid, confused, and sometimes at death's door. Mam would clean each one up, talking to it in a low voice, gently brushing out every knot and tangle, stroking them and calming their fears, carefully combing manes and tails that might never have been touched by a human before. The donkeys seemed to trust her and feel safe with her because she was welcoming them home. For a lost and sick donkey, the sanctuary was a paradise like they had never known.

Although Mam had her own worries, she projected an aura of tranquility, and the frightened and ill donkeys seemed to pick up on that. Whatever Mam needed or wanted the donkeys to do, she could apply gentle, almost invisible pressure and persuade them to do it.

That was Mam's way with Aran, with all of the donkeys, and with Dad, my sisters, and me. She made it look easy, and we didn't even know what she was doing because she was so quiet about it, but she managed our family's lives with strength and efficiency, everything done and taken care of. She held our family together.

Mam was the original donkey whisperer, and everything I know, I learned from her. My sister Helen has the gift too. She's on the same wavelength as the donkeys. She has the touch.

Mam could also outwork any farm worker or groom; she could put them, and me, to shame mucking out stables, hauling sacks of feed, moving bales of hay and straw, and getting the donkeys to do whatever she wanted them to do. All of this . . . and Mam took care of us four too. She may not have told us she loved us much, but she fed us and cared for us and kept us safe, even more fiercely than she cared for the donkeys.

Together, Dad and Mam continued to take in more and more donkeys; the need was great and the work flourished. Dad reckons that over the years they rescued more than ten thousand animals. When he retired and stepped down from running the sanctuary, Dad was inducted into the National Hall of Fame, acknowledged for his fifty-one years of caring for donkeys.

I wish I could give him and Mam an award for caring for his wild donkey of a son, as well. My family established a legacy of caring for animals who are forgotten, cruelly treated, or abandoned, and I grew up the beneficiary of their love, care, wisdom, and experience.

I'd seen and experienced the amount of energy my parents had poured into the sanctuary. We lived, ate, and slept the donkey sanctuary, and the sanctuary was like another brother or sister to us, requiring all of our attention.

The need was overwhelming, and yet somehow I'd gotten lost along the way. I was wandering in the wilderness, not wanting to be seen or helped, though my family and friends tried. It was going to take a miracle to get me home again.

CHAPTER ELEVEN

GUINNESS
The DONKEY

⊕

One drink is too many for me and a thousand not enough.

BRENDAN BEHAN

I'M OKAY. I'm still here. Brilliant. I don't know if it was the lingering effect of the anesthesia from the surgery or my general state of mind, but I was unfazed by what had happened in front of the Indian restaurant. I wasn't glad or relieved or grateful to be alive.

My feelings were . . . missing. The only feeling I could conjure up was confusion—how had my mam appeared when I got hurt? I knew it couldn't really have been her in the flesh, but it seemed so real. She had been right there with me, holding my hand.

I was released from the hospital two days later. They wanted to keep me longer, but I lived right across the street, so I persuaded them to let me go. My arm took a few weeks to heal, and I had to go back every day for a nurse to check the wound for infection and apply a fresh dressing. But the day after I was released, I was back in the pub drinking.

The one thing that did haunt me from the window experience was the look in the eyes of the man in the window. I didn't feel like the reflection was actually me—it seemed like a separate entity, and it was frightening to think about. The sight was seared into my mind—hollow eyes like a feral beast and black as night.

I'm glad Mam wasn't actually there to see that look, although maybe she'd seen it before. It was the look of death.

A donkey once came into the sanctuary with that same look, with the same black eyes. His name was Guinness. Not surprisingly, his owner ran a very busy pub in a rural part of County Mayo.

Every night, the owner gathered up all the bottles and cans and emptied whatever was left in them into the donkey's water trough. And every night, Guinness would drink all the slops, the leftover dregs from the bottoms of the glasses of that day's drinks. It's a tradition in Ireland to always leave an inch at the bottom of a pint of Guinness. A tipsy donkey sounds funny, but it was actually serious.

A bellyful of slops became a routine for the donkey, day in and day out, for over twenty years. Finally, the owner grew old and couldn't keep up the pub, so he retired and closed it down. No one knew what to do with the poor donkey, so he ended up at the donkey sanctuary.

From the minute his hooves hit the ground as he backed out of the horse box, Guinness began to act strangely. He was nervous and trembling, shaking his head, pawing at the ground, and acting like he was very uncomfortable. No one knew his background yet, but we called the former owner and he explained the situation. Then we knew—Guinness the donkey was a long-term alcoholic going through severe withdrawal. He was lost, confused, and angry because he didn't know where he was or why he was there.

The vet examined him, and Guinness seemed healthy overall, but starting from the first night, we could hear him going berserk in the barn, kicking and heaving himself around and crashing against the walls over and over again.

Everyone was afraid he'd seriously injure himself before it was

all over, so Dad told me to add extra straw to where Guinness bed-
ded down. I banked armloads of loose straw against all four corners
of his stall, but I was worried about him; we all were. You could see
madness in the donkey's eyes. They had a strange focus—glassy,
staring, and dark. So dark.

My sister Helen once told me she could tell if I was drunk by
my eyes—they were blank, like I wasn't there.

Guinness survived his detox, got sober, and became healthy
again. His eyes cleared up and lightened up, and he learned to be
satisfied with fresh, clear water. If he could do it, maybe my time
was coming too, because something needed to change. My demons
were taking over. My girlfriend didn't know what to do with my
behaviors and my moods and couldn't live with me. I didn't like
myself at all. I regretted everything and felt ashamed and useless.

With the baby on the way, we had both decided to move back to
nearby Buttevant. For me, it was yet another fresh start. My family
and friends welcomed me back, and I got a job driving a lorry
and making deliveries around Cork City. We rented a house and
settled in. We continued to fight and nothing much had changed
for me, but at least we were near family to help with the baby.

Then our son, Darragh, surprised us by arriving three months
early on November 12, 2004. He weighed just two pounds, and the
doctors at the hospital in Cork City weren't sure he would make it.

His legs were the size of my finger, and his skin was transparent.
You could see his internal organs and blood vessels. He seemed so
frail.

I was devastated, with emotions flooding in that I didn't know
how to handle, although I tried to hide my pain and keep it all
together. Whenever I left the hospital after visiting baby Darragh,
on my way home to Liscarroll I'd stop at St. Mary's Church in
Mallow, light a candle, then get on my knees in the last row of
pews and pray my heart out.

"God, what is going on?" I'd plead, tears streaming down my face. "Why have you put so much destruction in my path?"

I thought about Anita, the Valentine's Day crash in Lebanon, and now Darragh.

"Please. Help me."

I had reached the end of myself, and I reached out to God because there was nothing else to do.

I was strong, but I felt like I had finally broken. I'd had enough. My life was a nightmare full of the shakes, fevers, paranoia, hallucinations, walking blackouts, rage, and despair. I couldn't go on like this. I wanted to live. For Darragh.

I visited the church almost every single evening, and one night while I was praying, I noticed something new. A tickle in my heart, like when Aran met my gaze those many years ago on the island. I felt something deep inside, like a little ray of light breaking through the shadows.

"God, are you there?"

I wasn't sure, but maybe God *was* listening to my desperate prayers, because Darragh lived. We left the hospital with him on Christmas morning. As I carried him through the door of the hospital, we were met with a brass band stationed outside, playing Christmas tunes. Darragh woke up and started crying, and who could blame him? It was a rude and loud introduction to the outside world for such a tiny baby.

Soon enough, though, I started slipping back into the darkness and I began again to think about taking my own life, like I had when I first got out of the army. I wasn't doing anybody any good staying around. I even had something of a plan.

Halfway up the hill to the rock in the sanctuary was the massive, beautiful old oak tree above my grandmother's house. My sister Eileen and I had played there for countless hours as children, climbing the tree and running around under the canopy. Dad had made rope swings for each of us with a log tied at the bottom to sit on. We'd each get on one and launch ourselves way out over the meadow, or spin ourselves around until we got dizzy, or try to knock each other off by crashing in the middle.

The seats on the swings were long gone, but the ropes were still blowing in the Irish winds. It was there I could hang myself, with a view of the fields I loved and the rock just above at the top of the hill. I thought about it very hard one night in particular. I remember the cold breeze blowing the rope around. It was there—ready—a way to end my pain.

But one thing held me back. Darragh. He was just a few months old, and I'd be putting him and my family through hell when I was found. I just couldn't go through with it. I didn't want my son to grow up and discover what I had done. I was afraid that him knowing I'd ended my own life would cause him to inherit my pain.

⟿ ⟾

Six months later, my sister Debbie saw me at my worst. I had taken some ecstasy and was in the backyard, out of my mind. She dragged me to the car and took me on a long drive. "My brother isn't here anymore," she cried. "You're as good as dead. You need to go away somewhere and get help!"

For my family's sake, and especially Darragh's, I agreed to go to a drug and alcohol treatment center. I knew that if I didn't make a change, I wasn't going to see my Darragh grow up. I owed it to him to give it a try. I was tired . . . so, so tired. I wasn't sure I could fight anymore; the shadow man inside of me was winning. But maybe rehab would help.

The program was going to be five weeks long, and I was terrified. Everyone was worried that I wouldn't follow through. The day before I was supposed to go into treatment, I was in Buttevant at an all-day drinking session at the OK Corral with a good friend named Alan. There was much to celebrate at the pub. A feature film called *The Wind That Shakes the Barley*, an intense historical drama about the Irish War of Independence and the Civil War of the 1920s, was filming next door. Dad had lent the film company a donkey named Lucky Lady, and she acted her part like a star. Alan and I signed up to be extras. Our legs appeared on-screen, but you couldn't see our faces, which is probably good because we were already tipsy when we got on set.

At the OK Corral I was drinking fast and hard, very nervous about what was going to happen the next day at the treatment center. I didn't want to leave Darragh, and I didn't like the idea of being locked away somewhere doing God knows what. I also didn't know what my body was going to do without the drink.

After a while we left the pub in Buttevant, and we went to Mallow for another drinking session. Deep down I felt like I was at a major crossroads and this was my last hurrah. If I never got to drink again, I wanted to enjoy myself this last day before I got strapped into the straitjacket. Except I wasn't enjoying myself, of course. We drove past the church, found a spot to park, and sauntered into the pub.

We got our drinks, then I had a flash of inspiration. "Alan, there's nothing here for me anymore. Ireland's a mess."

Alan nodded and took another drink.

"I have an idea. Let's get out of here and go to England. Today. We can get off this godforsaken island and go somewhere else. What about joining the French Foreign Legion?"

I pulled out my phone, looked up the number for the bus station in Cork City, and started to call for the schedule.

"Well, I only have sixty pounds in my wallet," mumbled Alan.

Wait, I thought. *I'd better check my wallet.* I clicked off the call and pulled out my wallet. I had twenty pounds. That wasn't going to get me very far, but I wasn't ready to give up yet. I was scared and felt like running away, baby or not. *There has to be a way.*

I pulled my phone out again and decided to call my bank to see how much money was in my account. I pulled up the number, then when I heard the prompt, punched in my account number. I was hoping for good news, but my balance was zero.

I clicked off. "There goes that plan anyway, Alan." I took another drink. A group of girls sitting behind us got up to leave. They were happy and laughing as they hugged and gathered up their things. *Oh, to feel like that again.*

I had another idea. *Maybe I can get an overdraft*, I thought. *I might as well try; I have nothing to lose now.*

I got up from my bar stool and walked to a quieter part of the pub. I called the bank again, hoping I could talk someone into giving me some kind of loan. I stood next to a large tropical plant in a big pot and waited for someone in the loan department to come on the line.

The girls were gone, and the pub had quieted down. Out of the corner of my eye, I spotted something on the floor behind the plant. With the phone to my ear, I crouched about halfway down and looked. It was a small woman's purse. *What?*

My heart, numbed though it was, started picking up speed. Was this God? Was this the answer to my prayers?

I looked around, and no one seemed to be looking for the purse. Did it belong to one of those girls? I put my phone in my pocket and in the same motion, I reached down and picked up the purse and held it close, grabbed a nearby chair and turned it around, then sat with the purse in my lap and my back to the room. There was a thick roll of cash inside.

My heart started hammering. I was looking at salmon-colored notes, about a thousand euros I guessed.

*This money will help me get away from here. I'll get a fresh start.
This is my chance. Thank you, God.*

Quick as a flash, I slipped the money into my pocket. I shoved
the purse further down into the shadows behind the plant, then
got up and rejoined Alan at the bar. I grabbed my drink, feeling
like my head was about to explode. "I can't believe it," I murmured.

Alan looked at me quizzically.

I sat there trying to be calm, thinking of all the things I could
do with that money. It was like a gift, like finding a pot of treasure
in a field. Nothing like this had ever happened to me before. *It's
some kind of sign.*

About five minutes had passed when a girl came rushing into
the pub, close to hysterics. "Where's my purse? I can't find it. I've
lost my purse," she said as she rushed around, looking under tables
and chairs. "I'm sure I left it here. Have you seen it?" she asked
the barmaid.

I sat and listened, acting like nothing was going on, as she
searched frantically. The girl came over and stood behind us. "Did
you see anything?" she asked.

"Uh, no." I shook my head with a small, regretful smile. "I'm
sorry."

The barmaid came out and helped her look, and when they
couldn't find the purse, the girl started sobbing and ran down the
hall to the bathroom, slamming the door behind her.

I put my hand inside my pocket and wrapped it around the
money.

I'd gotten away with it. I was sure the girl would leave after she
finished crying in the bathroom. She'd looked all over the room
and had asked everyone. After she left, I would wait for a few
minutes, finish my drink, get up, and walk slowly out.

No one would ever know.

CHAPTER TWELVE

SANCTUARY

Faith without works is dead.

JAMES 2:26, NASB

THE MINUTES DRAGGED BY. I didn't see the girl. She was either in a hallway somewhere, or maybe she was still in the bathroom. She didn't seem to suspect anyone in the pub.

Her friends didn't know what had happened. The barmaid didn't know. No one knew.

Except for me. I knew.

There was a part of me that suddenly dug in its heels, like a stubborn old donkey, and stopped. When a donkey decides to stop walking, there's not much you can do to get it going again. Donkeys have even been known to sit back on their haunches when they don't want to do something. You just have to wait.

I was still full of drink, but for some reason I had a moment of clarity. *What am I going to do? Walk out the door with someone else's money?*

I'd been raised to respect the possessions of others, and in this moment, my conscience seemed to rise up and come alive, at least a bit.

Still, I was scared. I decided the minute I got out of the door I'd start running down the street with the money. I wanted to get away from the pub and the distraught girl.

What then? Will I go to the bus station, buy that ticket, and start the journey to London and parts beyond? I'd be leaving baby Darragh. I couldn't do it.

What if rehab will actually work? I didn't have a whole lot of confidence that I was going to win my battle with alcohol, but what was my alternative?

All of this went circling round and round my head, and in the end, all I could think was, *I can't do this. This isn't me.*

Then I heard her voice in the hallway, so upset. This time something in her voice got to me.

I retrieved the purse, shoved the money back inside, and headed to the hallway. The girl was down at the far end, standing with a friend. I approached, holding out the purse.

"Where did you find it?" she asked, her eyes wide open in surprise.

"You didn't look around the back of the plant," I lied. "Look, you have it back now."

I sat back down at the bar with Alan, and in a minute, she walked back in, stepped up to the bar, and bought drinks for us both.

I took a sip of my new drink.

"My company gave me a thousand euros as a bonus," she said with relief. "I'm going to Australia." She smiled, then sat down at the bar. It was awkward, to say the least. *Did she know?*

In the end it was a very close call. I could have been caught, which would have resulted in a bad outcome. But if I wasn't caught it would have been even worse—because I would have left Ireland again. I would have run out on my family. Even worse, I would have abandoned baby Darragh.

Once again the story of the devil tempting Jesus in the desert flashed across my mind. Maybe this had been God's test for me.

There were times I felt like a kid in a man's body, throwing tantrums. Maybe I was. I'd started drinking so early in life, and at times I felt like my emotions were still those of an adolescent. I didn't have a strong sense of self. I didn't really know who I was—or who I would be when I was sober. I didn't understand responsibility, and yet I needed to learn how to be responsible, at least for my son.

Tomorrow was a new day, and the start of a new life, I hoped. I had made an important choice—to stay with Darragh and build a family of my own.

It's time to grow up, Patrick.

The next day I gave Darragh hugs and kisses and left for the twenty-eight-day program at a facility in County Tipperary called Aiseiri, which means "to rise again," *resurrection* in Irish.

No one really knew where I was going except for close family. My boss must have wondered where I disappeared to. It was a big secret, hard to keep in such a small village, but the Irish are used to keeping secrets.

To be honest, my memories of the program are something of a blur. I went through withdrawals under medical supervision, and I couldn't sleep for the first week. I remember looking out the bathroom window at the night sky, at the same stars and moon I used to look at from the rock or over in Lebanon, as I sang the "Galtee Mountain Boy," Mam's favorite.

There were counselors and group work, and there were times I felt the presence of God there. I was fascinated by the work the counselors did.

I finished the program, then returned to Liscarroll, where my recovery began. I was twenty-six years old and sober for the first time since childhood. So much had happened to me in my short life and so much needed to change. I remember lying in bed at Mam and Dad's house and feeling overwhelmed, with all the thoughts and emotions I'd been anesthetizing with drink coming to life and flooding through me. My body, mind, heart, and spirit all needed to recover. I felt a little lost. *What am I going to do? What is my purpose in life?*

I needed more of a goal than trying to get married and have children. I'd learned that becoming a dad wouldn't magically solve all my problems. There had to be more to it. Now that I'd had my first taste of sobriety, I wanted to start living and stop existing.

Then a notion popped into my head, out of nowhere. *I think I'd like to help other people. I want to be a counselor.* If I had said it out loud, everyone would have thought I was joking because I was still a mess. I had no idea how it would ever happen, because I had no money and nowhere to go. I knew I needed to stay in a supportive environment—running away hadn't done me any good—so I hoped to stay in the village for a while.

Dad took pity on me and offered me a job again back at the Donkey Sanctuary, after getting clearance from Dr. Svendsen in England. I didn't have to go through an interview. "Your family is like my family," she told Dad. "We must look after him."

It was an act of great mercy, because no one else would have taken me. I was unemployable. I was a real-life prodigal son, who decided to turn his back on his family and squander every opportunity he'd been given. In the biblical story, when the rebellious son returns, instead of greeting him with anger and shaming, his father greets him with open arms and a welcome-back celebration. He didn't deserve this kind of homecoming whatsoever, but his father loved him so much he did it anyway. In fact, when he saw his lost son coming, he *ran* to meet him.

When Dad offered me a job, he was welcoming me back into the family, into his life's work, and into the sanctuary. Just as Mam and Dad opened their arms and their hearts to broken donkeys, they opened their arms and hearts one more time to their broken son. Everyone in Liscarroll now knew what was going on too.

Dad knew I was going to have to start from scratch, just like we did with the new donkeys coming in for the first time. The hard, physical work would be good for me. I would be outside with the animals, and the activity would tire me out. I was in the midst of a rescue, only this time I was the donkey.

When a rescued donkey comes in, first there's a veterinary assessment to take care of any health issues, especially their feet. Some donkeys came in with what we called "Aladdin's shoes" (or slipper feet), a condition where the hooves are never trimmed and overgrown. They grow so long they actually curl forward and keep growing until they point forward instead of backward and stick up in the air like a fancy slipper from *The Arabian Nights*. It's terribly painful for the animal, and sometimes a donkey will lie down and refuse to get up because it's no longer possible for them to walk without excruciating pain. There can be permanent damage to the bones, ligaments, and tendons, and sometimes it's irreversible.

After their feet were examined, new donkeys were started on a healthy diet tailored to their nutritional needs and given fresh water. Then came detailed grooming, removing knots and tangles, foreign objects and parasites, paying careful attention to detangling and brushing out the coat, mane, and tail. Some donkeys needed shearing if their coat was long and badly matted or covered in parasites. All new donkeys were isolated for six full weeks, giving the veterinarian time to conduct thorough health examinations.

Finally, we began socialization, scratching the special pressure points on their backs and necks and behind their ears, getting them used to people, and then placing them with other donkeys to form bonds and work them into a herd.

In time, most donkeys can heal if they're given the chance. I hoped this was going to be my story too. Mam and Dad had started a sanctuary for lost and hurt donkeys. I was a lost soul and needed sanctuary too.

I could relate to the intake process of the donkeys I was helping with—I was a mess, I was in isolation, and I needed plenty of observation and treatment for a successful recovery.

Every time I went to work and walked up the hill past the oak tree with the rope hanging down, a shiver went through my body. *Not today.*

About six months into my recovery, I was with Helen at the sanctuary when a donkey came in with slipper feet. After a veterinary examination, it was determined the poor donkey's feet were too far gone—putting her down was the kindest thing to do. The vet gave her the injection, and we left the donkey with its bonded friend, giving the grieving friend time to process.

. We came back about a half hour later, and when we peeked inside the stall, the friend had a grip on the dead donkey's collar and was trying to pick her up and get her to stand on her feet. It was heartbreaking to watch the devotion and the grief, and I was suddenly flooded with a torrent of emotion. I felt so strongly for this poor donkey and for her friend processing the loss. I was overwhelmed with grief, and I began to weep. I'd buried my feelings and numbed myself with substances for so long that it felt like an awakening. I was experiencing normal human emotions again, like I had with Aran all those years ago.

I wish with everything in me that this was the end of the story, that the fairy tale wound to a close with a happily-ever-after ending at the sanctuary, and that I went off on my merry way through the green hills of Liscarroll with a big beautiful Irish rainbow arcing over my head and a donkey at my side. But I wasn't a little kid anymore, with Aran keeping me company and Mam making sure I had everything I needed. This wasn't the fairy-tale ending. And the rainbow was lost in the storm clouds somewhere far above.

Not even a full year later, I broke out drinking again. I kept working at the sanctuary and trying to hold it together for Darragh, but the unhealthy patterns resurfaced. I was much more comfortable with the self-destructive life I'd known for so long than I was with the sober life. There was relationship drama, more car crashes, and more time in the courts. It was like a bad rerun of the life I thought I'd left behind when I returned that purse and went to rehab.

I had a new girlfriend, and she became the mother of my second son, Patrick. He was born on September 6, five years after Darragh, in the same hospital in Cork City.

To my horror, little Patrick was born with no pulse, not breathing, flatlined. They were able to get his heart started and get him breathing again, but we were warned of the possibility of permanent damage. I was beside myself.

I followed almost the same routine I'd established after Darragh was born. After work at the sanctuary, I'd drive to the hospital, visit baby Patrick, and then on the way home stop at the church in Mallow. I'd walk the path to the front door and go in, light a candle, then get on my knees in the last row of pews and pray for Patrick. This time, I was even more desperate. God had answered my prayers for Darragh, so maybe he would answer them for little Patrick too.

"God, are you there? Are you real? I need your help. Patrick needs your help."

I didn't pray for myself, because I didn't feel like I deserved help. I had already had some help when I went to rehab, with follow-ups afterward. Even though I'd had the chance, I'd messed it up.

But I *could* pray for Patrick, and I prayed hard. I loved my two boys more than anything or anyone I'd ever loved before. I knew I needed to get myself together so I could be a good father to both of them. Every time I prayed, I vowed to become a better father and a better man. I wanted to love my boys and I wanted to feel loved too.

I remembered when I was praying for Darragh as a baby that something had stirred inside of me, as if a tiny bit of light was breaking through. I hoped for that same feeling as I petitioned God on Patrick's behalf.

While my life was still chaotic and messy, I was forming a new habit—going to God and asking him for help. I only prayed like that when I was desperate, but it was a positive new pattern for me, and I was relieved when Patrick came home.

My PTSD had not improved much since I'd left London and returned to Ireland. The unpredictable fear, anxiety, depression, and paranoia ruled my life, and I didn't know what to do with it. My relationship with Patrick's mother faltered, and I felt like I was falling back into the darkness again. I had traumatic memories on endless, vivid loops that ran in my head, and I didn't know how to deal with the ups and downs of life. The traumas I'd experienced were still there, living on inside of me, keeping me from moving forward and learning how to be responsible and find my purpose in life.

One night I couldn't sleep and I went out on the landing of the house, pacing up and down and around for hours—all night long—walking around in circles. I wasn't drunk, I was just adrift, going nowhere. And the light inside me was barely flickering as the darkness encroached. I had a sense that the end was near for me, although I didn't know how or when. I just knew it was coming. Yet I kept trying to work, to keep up a routine, and to be there for my boys after Patrick got home from the hospital. Despite everything I tried to do, my relationship with Patrick's mom ended, and I was alone again.

Two failed relationships made me believe I might never have a family, and I felt like an utter failure. I wondered what people thought of me and I didn't see a way out.

I wanted to try something new, so I went to Dublin and tried performing some stand-up comedy. My donkey calls were the star of the routine, but I also told profanity-laced stories about my life, about the army, and about the donkeys. People laughed and seemed to enjoy it, even though it was dark humor and said with bitterness.

How ironic to be doing comedy and making others happy when I didn't know the first thing about happiness. I was still playing the clown, trying to get people to like me, trying to make them laugh.

There was one good thing that came out of it: The storytelling forced me to take a look at my life and my journey. But looking back on it, I was usually drunk on stage and the audience was probably laughing at the way I was acting as much or more than at my actual jokes and stories. Here's one of my jokes:

Did you hear about the carrot that died?
There was a big turnip at his funeral.

The next few years were a blur as I replayed unhealthy old patterns. Dad and Mam and sometimes my sisters picked up the slack and helped take care of the boys when I was out drinking. I lived in a house next door to Mam and Dad with some roommates from the village, and soon villagers started complaining about our behavior. I still had my job at the Donkey Sanctuary, but I wasn't sure how much longer I could hold on to it, between my addiction and my PTSD.

When Darragh was seven and Patrick was two, Dad and Mam went on holiday to see family in Cardiff, Wales, when he suffered a serious heart attack. We knew it was bad—after all, his father had dropped dead in a field from a heart attack—so my sister Debbie and I traveled across the Irish Sea to be with Mam at the hospital.

Dad had been lucky that it had happened while he was still at the hotel, right next door to the hospital. He needed emergency cardiac surgery.

I had a bad feeling about the outcome, and as usual, I stayed out all night drinking. In the morning I got a call that Dad wasn't doing well. After the surgery, his heart had stopped and they had to use the defibrillator to bring him back. The situation was dire.

Debbie had already returned home by then, but Mam, Helen (who had arrived separately), and I raced to the hospital at about 6:30 in the morning. I was arguing with them in the car, drunk and hung over, angrily hitting the steering wheel. When we arrived, to my shame I couldn't bring myself to go into Dad's room. I felt like I hadn't been a good son, always full of anger and arguing with him. Even though I was scared that I was about to lose him, I couldn't go in and face him because I hadn't made things right.

I left the hospital and went back out to the car. I waited there alone while Mam and Helen stayed inside with him.

Dad was in the hospital for weeks recovering—he had a near-death experience and said God saved his life and brought him back—but what stayed with me was my utter failure to be with him during his darkest, most difficult time. I will never forget that feeling. If Dad had not survived, I would have missed saying a proper goodbye.

When he had recovered, Dad and Mam came back from Wales and settled back into their house at the sanctuary.

But his near-death experience changed something for me. If Dad had been given a second chance at life, maybe there was another chance for me, too.

I'd had enough. I couldn't tame my mind or heart, and every bad thing I'd ever done, every hard thing that had ever happened to me, wouldn't leave me alone. If I didn't get some help, I knew I couldn't make it much longer.

One night I walked out the back door and made my way through the damp, dark fields of the sanctuary. It was cold, but the clouds had blown away and the stars were shimmering in clusters and streams across the deep, dark sky. I noticed the stars for a moment, but then I went inward again and the stars faded away.

I could hear the donkeys munching inside the barn as I passed by. They'd already eaten dinner, but they stood knee-deep in fresh, clean straw I'd spread around just a few hours before, and they loved nibbling in the quiet with their friends.

I wished I had Aran or Timmy with me at that moment, but I knew I needed to do this alone. I also knew that if I didn't, there would be no hope for me. I climbed up the hill I used to climb every day on the way to school, trying not to think about the old oak over to the right. Up toward the top, I passed by a line of shrubs and then I was in the open space at the crown of the hill.

Years ago, Dad had fenced off the rock and created a space for donkeys, with a walkway around it for visitors. I followed that fence now, first to the right and then along the circular path around to the left. I couldn't see the rock to my left or the castle below to my right, but I knew they were there. I could see them in my mind's eye. I could sense their presence.

My breathing started to speed up as I walked. My anxiety and pain were building again, even here in my favorite place, my most sacred place. If I couldn't find peace here, where would I ever find it? My thoughts and dreams and memories and feelings tumbled around inside me, like a pack of wild dogs fighting each other, and I felt pressure rising inside my head.

At the end of the walk I stopped, leaned forward, and rested my hands on the fence. My head dropped down. I couldn't see anything but the ground in front of me, which seemed to rise up and penetrate my body and soul like an icy black cloud. I closed my eyes and gripped the railing.

"I need help."

I took a deep breath, and with the rock at my back and the ancient castle in front of me below, I breathed out the words again.

"I need help!"

Then I was crying out, no longer just saying the words to myself, telling myself I needed help, but crying out to someone else. It had to be God.

"Are you there, God? I need help. I need you to prove yourself to me!"

My heart and soul and everything inside me that still had some life and energy screamed out silently under those stars.

"If you're here, help me! I don't know how much longer I can last."

I didn't know if anyone heard me, but I felt a little better just asking. The stars looked a little brighter, too, when I finally opened my eyes.

Below the hill, sitting on a stone wall, a woman was praying. She was under those same stars, praying for her future husband. She didn't know who he was, just that he was out there somewhere.

We were just a few hundred feet away, completely unaware of each other's presence, but God was watching and listening. He was already at work.

CHAPTER THIRTEEN

UHEN DONKEYS
TALK

God's help is nearer than the door.

IRISH PROVERB

FARMING IN IRELAND can be a challenge for older folk. When a farmer's aging legs aren't as strong as they used to be, it can be tough to climb the steep hills and get the work done, especially in wet weather.

This was true for Pat, a farmer whose land was adjacent to the sanctuary, after he had knee replacement surgery. Pat had an energetic sheep dog with one blue eye and one green eye who was more than capable of herding the flock. But even with the dog's help, Pat couldn't get around the hills well enough to move his sheep so soon after the surgery.

One workday I was up on the hill at the sanctuary and looked across to see Pat in his field. The old farmer was in his car, driving slowly but strategically around the grassy field, chasing his sheep. That was funny enough, but as I watched, I saw something I'd never seen before. Pat's dog was in the passenger seat of the car! His shaggy head was hanging out the passenger window with his tongue lolling. He was having a great time keeping an eye on the sheep from the comfort of the car, letting out a bark now and again.

I had to admit Pat drove with a masterful touch, pulling sharp U-turns up and down the hills. The sheep seemed to understand exactly what was going on and were fully signed on with the new program.

Sometimes guidance and direction don't look like what you expect. While the sheep probably weren't anticipating being rounded up by an automobile, they seemed to know how to follow, even if the shepherd and his dog were doing it in an unconventional way.

I was learning this lesson too. Help, guidance, encouragement, and direction started coming from unexpected places. There was something happening behind the scenes, starting to push back the darkness and let in some tiny splinters of light. I needed to learn how to pay attention to that divine guidance for my journey and listen to the wisdom of others who knew the way.

Balaam's donkey is a good example of wisdom. Who would ever think of listening to a donkey for direction about which path to take and how to stay safe? But it made sense to me. I'd been listening to donkeys since I was a lad, and they had been listening to me.

Mam had read us the Bible story of Balaam, a man who was hired by others to lay blessings and curses on people. Two tribal chieftains wanted to curse the people of Israel, so they hired Balaam to deliver one of his curses. The night before, Balaam had a dream from God, who warned him directly: "Do not go . . . you are not to curse these people, for they have been blessed."

You'd think Balaam would listen. But he didn't because he'd been offered too much money not to go.

I could relate completely. How many times had people who cared about me told me to mind myself, and I didn't listen?

As Balaam traveled to deliver the curse, something very strange happened. He was riding his donkey when suddenly she stopped in the middle of the road. The donkey could see what Balaam could not: The angel of the Lord, with mighty sword drawn, was facing them and blocking their passage.

The donkey knew what was about to happen, so she did what any wise donkey would do. She bolted and ran into a field. Balaam was furious and beat her with his wood staff, then grabbed her reins and yanked her back to the road.

The donkey looked up and saw that the angel was gone, so when Balaam got on her back, she started moving again. But a few minutes later, the road narrowed between stone walls on each side, just like an Irish road. Once again, the angel stood in the middle of the road. But the donkey didn't want another beating, so she broke into a trot and tried to slip between the angel and the stone wall. The space was big enough for the donkey, but not for Balaam. She crushed his foot against the wall and then made another run for it.

Balaam was enraged and his foot was hurting so he hit the donkey again, forcing her to go forward. They continued on a little farther. And then, for the third time, the angel appeared in front of Balaam's donkey.

This time there was no way around the angel, so the donkey gave up, curled her legs up under her, and laid down with Balaam still in the saddle. Once again, he hit her in anger.

The donkey couldn't be silent anymore. With God's help, she spoke up. "What have I done to you that deserves your beating me three times?"

"You've made me look foolish," Balaam shouted, standing over her. "I would kill you right now if I had a sword."

"But I'm the same donkey who has faithfully carried you for your entire life," she said. "Have I ever done anything like this before?"

Balaam shook his head, ashamed of what he had done. Then God opened his eyes and he saw an angel standing right in front of him, sword drawn, ready to be used.

Balaam bowed his head and fell to the ground, face first.

This time it was the angel's turn to talk. "Why did you beat your donkey? Look, I blocked your way because you were stubbornly resisting me. The donkey saw me each time and shied away; otherwise, I would certainly have killed you . . . and spared the donkey."[2]

It was a wakeup call for Balaam, a man blinded by power and money, who wasn't listening to the voice of God. He hadn't paid attention to his donkey's cues either.

It's a powerful story about how a donkey could see even when the man known for his prophetic powers couldn't. Balaam was valued for his ability to use words to curse and to bless, but he was schooled by the words of his donkey, who he thought was a dumb animal who didn't know what she was doing and certainly couldn't talk. In the end, this supposedly learned and accomplished man was taught by his donkey about the value of watching, listening, and paying attention to those who are sent to guide us, help us, and care for us, whether it's a donkey or a human.

I had not been good at this either. I was guilty of filtering out and ignoring those around me as I went down my own path. I thought I knew what I was doing, but like Balaam, I had proved myself more of an ass than any donkey. And I knew there was a sword out there somewhere, waiting for me.

Since my relationship with both Darragh's mother and Patrick's

<hr>

[2] Adapted from Numbers 22:7-33.

mother had broken up, it was just me alone again. I did my job at the sanctuary the best I could, took care of the boys when I had them, and tried to keep my drinking from ruining our lives.

⊰═◦ ◦═⊱

Throughout the next few months a battle raged inside me. I'd asked God for help and part of me was waiting for it. But I was still drinking on the weekends, even when I had the boys. Sometimes Mam would watch them for me or Helen would help out. I didn't always know where the boys were staying or what was happening because after more than a few pints at the pub, I'd show up at Mam and Dad's in the middle of the night. I'd sleep off my binge on the sitting room sofa while life went on around me. Helen told me later she kept her kids out of the front room when I was there, not because she didn't want to disturb me, but because she didn't want her kids to see me like that.

In September of that year, I ran into Mary, my friend Sean Murphy's mother, outside of Philip Egan's pub on a fine Sunday morning. I was already very drunk.

"Mary, I'd love to be a counselor like you," I said.

She smiled and somehow didn't act surprised at my words. "I'll get back to you Monday morning."

Mary was true to her word and dropped by the next day to give me a pamphlet about a program at an organization called the Flatstone Institute. I gathered up my courage and signed up for a personal development course called "Steps on My Journey," created by Marie Stuart and Ann Parfrey.

The course was the first step before a four-year program of psychotherapy training. As strange as it might seem, I still dreamed of becoming a counselor even though I couldn't get myself together, hanging on to my tattered dream to learn how to help others.

But after Dad's heart attack I wasn't sure if I could still attend. I hadn't contacted the leaders after I first signed up like I was supposed to. Then Marie Stuart herself called to see if I was still planning to come.

"I won't be going on any course," I told her. "My dad had a heart attack and almost died."

"Well, Patrick, it might be the right time for you to take the course," she said. There was something about her voice and her manner that made me feel like she cared. She listened as I tried to explain why I couldn't come.

"I will keep the chair empty for you and if you come back in time, the chair will be ready for you," Marie said firmly, then bade me goodbye.

A few days later, I phoned her and said I would be there. I wanted my relationship with my father to get better, and I was hoping the course would help. The personal development course was a program to teach strategies and frameworks for personal growth, goal setting, self-discipline, and self-improvement.

"I held the chair for you," she said. I could hear her smile.

Even though I was thirty-three years old in the year of our Lord, in many ways I was still an immature boy who was trying to learn how to function as an adult after so many years of drinking. I needed to learn how to grow up and take care of myself because I had two boys to care for. I was still struggling in many parts of my life, and I hoped the course would help me move forward and be a step toward my tentative dream of becoming a counselor.

Marie did not look like a typical nun; she was a strong-looking woman from West Clare who served in the Sisters of Mercy. She had a high position in the order, but she wasn't dressed in a nun's habit. Marie wore street clothes, had short silvery hair and eyes that seemed especially intense, like she could see into my soul. Yet she was quick to smile. She came across as humble, straightforward, and no-nonsense.

All three instructors—Alan Davis, Ann Parfrey, and Marie—were just brilliant from the start. Alan was kind and welcoming. On the first weekend retreat at the Nano Nagle Center, Ann told me I would make a great counselor. And Marie? Well, her influence has been immeasurable.

The weekly program wasn't easy; we met together, then broke into discussion groups of four, then came back together into the big group again. I probably kept going because of Marie—there was something about her that kept me feeling like I needed to be there. A bond quickly formed between us and I almost felt like she knew everything about me, even though she couldn't have. She seemed to be able to see all of me, both the surface and the shadows.

That fall, while I was in the program, Mam and Dad let me move back in with them to save money. My job at the sanctuary wasn't going well, with my frequent absences or late arrival times straining my relationship with my boss. I was worried about money and wasn't sure I'd even have enough to buy Christmas presents for Darragh and Patrick.

One particularly bad week in November, wracked with anxiety, I left Mam and Dad's on a Sunday evening and headed for a nightclub in Mallow, driving past the church where I had prayed for both of my sons. A couple of hours later I left the club and went to The Olde Fiddle pub next door. Two sisters from the village, Evelyn and Joanne O'Donovan, worked there, and it was a comfortable and familiar place. I stayed until six o'clock the next morning. After my last drink, I went to the toilet and came back into the pub to say goodbye.

As I caught my reflection in one of the panes of glass in the door, a strange thought crossed my mind. *No, I can't do this anymore.*

It had been a weekend full of heaviness and feelings of failure and shame. I couldn't shake the dark mood, and I felt like the time was coming where I might have to check myself into the hospital because I couldn't seem to calm myself down or escape the endless, anxious thoughts. They never stopped, and sooner or later they were going to knock me down and kill me. My days were numbered; I was sure of it.

Is this ever going to end? Am I going insane?

On Wednesday, there was a message on my phone from my supervisor at the donkey sanctuary, requesting to meet with me the very next day for a disciplinary hearing. With two reprimands already on my record for not showing up for work, he'd had enough and now my job was on the line. Two strikes, and now this was the third. It was a strong, hard dose of reality. Was I about to lose my job? I didn't want Mam and Dad to know because it was utterly humiliating that I couldn't hold down a job at the sanctuary my parents had started. It was about the worst thing that could happen. I had no other job options, no other plans. It felt like the end of the road.

As it happened, I had group that night in Cork City with Marie and the others. On the way to the meeting, my mind went around in circles.

Why am I this way? Why can't I keep my life together?

All I could think about was the mess my life had become, and what I'd be facing at tomorrow's meeting. There didn't seem to be any way out or any way forward for me. I was not only broke financially, but broken emotionally. When I opened the door to the classroom, I was in a near-panic. I sat down, nervously bouncing my leg up and down.

Marie greeted us and started the session. There were sixteen of us. Every few minutes, I looked at the clock on the wall. *How am I going to get through this?*

My mind was going a million kilometers a minute and I couldn't concentrate. Marie could have been speaking Russian for all I got out of it. Finally, I couldn't stand it any longer and I jumped up and headed for the door. I needed out.

"Paddy, are you okay?" asked Marie. Her eyes were filled with concern.

"Not really, Marie. Look, I've had enough. I'm not for this course." I already had my hand on the door handle, and I grabbed it so hard the metal bit into my palm. The pain helped me focus on what she was saying.

"Fair enough, Paddy." Her voice sounded a bit sad. "It's been nice to meet you. I wish you all the good luck in the future."

I froze for a minute. *What is going on?* Then I heard Marie again. "Paddy, where are ye?"

"Cork."

"No. Where are ye?"

"I'm in Cork." I let go of the lever, and my hand dropped to my side. I took a deep breath and let it out slowly. *I don't understand. What is she asking? What does she want?*

"No. Where *are* ye?"

I turned around to face her and the group. Marie's voice seemed to flow through me, front to back. I could sense her patience and feel her love for me. It was the same tickle in my heart I had experienced with Aran, and the feeling I used to get when I was praying for my boys at the church in Mallow.

But it was hard to accept this kind of soul connection from a real person, a woman of the church, and someone whom I didn't know very well at all. I wasn't used to it, and it was confusing. *Why would she care about me like this when she barely knows me? She doesn't know all that I've done or about the darkness in me.*

And yet I think she did, because she was somehow looking into my soul, seeing all of my pain, hopelessness, and shame. She saw me for who I truly was—someone who had pretended to be strong and yet was wounded and vulnerable from the hurts that had built up over so very many years.

I felt like a very young boy again, the boy Aran saw on the island. My defenses gave way and I started crying. My tears quickly turned into weeping, and my legs collapsed. I crumpled to the floor. I felt lost and alone—all the feelings that had haunted me for so long.

Then I heard footsteps.

CHAPTER FOURTEEN

ᚈINY ᚈINSEL

⊕

The Journey toward God is finished.
The Journey with God begins!

FROM A MUSLIM REFUGEE,

AS TOLD TO LINDA HARVEY KELLEY

MARIE REACHED DOWN and gently touched my shoulder. I felt her kindness. She saw me, she knew what I was all about, and she still cared.

Her touch broke through my mental haze, and I put out my hand. She lifted me up (don't ask me how an older gray-haired nun lifted me up from the ground, but she did), and she walked with me back to the center of the room. I had no idea what was going to happen, but I knew she did and I trusted her.

Marie gathered everyone around me, then she stood in front of me. "Close your eyes, Paddy." The rest of them laid their hands on my back and shoulders.

I was very still and at peace. It was like I had reached that point of no return and everything I'd ever done or been a part of was already behind me. The situation felt very right in that moment in time and I let myself trust . . . a new feeling for me.

Then Marie began to speak words of truth and goodness and love that came out of the wisdom and power of someone who belonged to God. The words poured out of her in a quiet, calm stream that washed over and pooled around me.

I wish I could remember the actual words she said. I wish I had a recording or could write them down to read them again. But maybe it doesn't matter. What is important is the way Marie talked to me, the way she held me, and the way she hadn't let me go.

She sees me. She really sees me for who I am.

"Marie, I'm cracked. I'm just cracked," I cried out.

"Those cracks can let the light in," said Marie.

I was reeling and I didn't know what to think of any of this. Maybe it was better if I didn't think, just opened my heart and freed my spirit to receive this gift.

The room felt charged with a strange sort of energy, almost sacred. It was like God had entered the room through Marie's hands, voice, and spirit, and I felt as if I was on holy ground.

In that moment, standing in the middle of the room with Marie and the others, something awoke inside of me. It's hard to describe what's going on in your soul, but the only way I can put it into words is this: Something broke open and broke free inside of me. Something was lifted away from me, and I rose up.

Because much of my life was defined by drink, and I had pushed all my feeling into some dark place, I was like a cork submerged in a murky liquid in a bottle, trapped and held down in the darkness where I couldn't see or breathe or get out.

All of a sudden, I was released and popped up to the surface, set free. It felt like a new beginning, as if I had been given new eyes, and for the first time I had awakened and could look up and see the light.

The date was November 24, 2012. I consider it my second birthday because it was the beginning of a new life for me.

And that drink at The Olde Fiddle just a couple of days before? It was the last drink I ever had.

◆──○ ○──◆

The next day I was utterly exhausted. But I was also, strangely, at peace.

I went into the disciplinary hearing with my supervisor, accompanied by a notetaker, at the donkey sanctuary. I wanted to be open and speak the truth, but I knew it wasn't going to be easy. I had said a prayer that morning that gave me a new sort of confidence. The outcome was going to be in God's hands.

I did something very odd for a disciplinary meeting. Instead of waiting to be questioned and having to defend myself, I decided to take the lead and asked to talk first.

"Before you start the meeting, I need to tell you something. I need to talk honestly to ye . . . I was wrong, and I'm sorry. I know there's a lot of people frustrated with me. I apologize for my behavior." I took a slow breath. Then I said it. "I have a problem with drinking." I stopped, looked my supervisor in the eye, and waited for his response.

Silence.

He seemed shocked. I knew it was because I had never once talked like this before. It was the first time I could ever remember humbling myself and saying those words.

He just let me talk. The notetaker stopped writing and, with eyes wide, listened.

"Look, all I can say is my love is for the animal. I love working here. It is my home. I don't want to leave."

It was the first time I'd been completely honest in a work situation for as long as I could remember—no storytelling, no exaggeration, and no trying to make myself look good. I owned up to my mistakes, and I would wait to see what would happen next. I put myself and my job in God's hands.

I don't think they could comprehend what was happening in the room. I know I couldn't. I felt a real power in the room that day. And just like with Marie, they listened.

When the meeting was over, I walked outside and started up the hill to the rock. Everything looked different, new, and brighter. I marveled at the green of the fields, the grays of the clouds, and the multicolored coats of the donkeys grazing around me. It was like I'd never seen any of this before. When I got to the top and walked the path that circled around the rock, I was overwhelmed. The world seemed fresh and clean and beautiful in a way I couldn't remember experiencing before. Or, at least since I was a lad. Even the rock looked clearer, the edges sharper.

How long have I been away from all of this? How long have I been blind?

I came to the end of the path, then stopped and leaned against the fence in the same place where I'd called out to God for help. I watched as the sun settled down behind the hills and the evening's colors streamed across the sky.

Thank you.

⋅⟶⟵⋅

An hour later my supervisor called and gave me his verdict. He would give me another chance! But he was stern. "This is your last warning." Now it was my turn to listen, and my heart thumped hard. I had another chance!

About two weeks into my new life without the drink, I was at Mam and Dad's, getting ready to hop in the car and head up the road to visit Helen, Timmy, and their two daughters, Sarah and Gemma.

Darragh was getting ready for bed. I told him I was going to Auntie Helen's. I could tell by the look on his face that he thought I was lying, but I didn't say anything more. When I got in the car, Darragh's expression haunted me and I thought, *What am I doing?*

I got out of the car, went inside the house, and found him lying on his side in the bed, staring at the wall with a blank look on his face.

"Are you okay, Darragh? Do you want to come to Auntie Helen's with me?"

"Yes!" He jumped out of the bed and into my arms. I got his jacket and wrapped it around him, still in his pajamas, then we walked to the car and got inside.

"Is everything alright, Darragh?" I started up the car and pulled out of the driveway.

"Yeah, Daddy. Everything's good."

"You looked a bit worried in the bedroom."

"Well, Daddy, I just thought you were going out to meet your friends tonight." His voice was quiet and matter-of-fact. "Then I wouldn't get to see you all weekend because you'd be sick on the couch."

Something grabbed at my heart and a cold chill went down my spine. That same black cloud by the rock the night I contemplated ending my life was here in the car with me for a moment. With us. Tears came to my eyes and my throat tightened, but I didn't want to let it show. I didn't want to frighten Darragh.

We arrived at Helen's a few minutes later. As we pulled up, Helen was standing at the front door. Darragh got out, and she gave him a hug before he went inside the house. Helen looked at me, still in the car, with a questioning look in her eyes. Then with a sister's intuition she shut the door to leave me be.

I began to weep inside the car, with the lights still on, for ten or fifteen minutes. It was the first time I realized the impact my drinking had had on Darragh.

I felt like my heart was breaking as I started to come to terms with what kind of father I had been. I saw myself for who I was, and I didn't want to be that person anymore.

I thought about all the times I had failed Darragh and Patrick, by losing jobs, losing my house, losing both of their mothers. When I was at the pubs, I knew they asked Mam where I was, and now I knew what she told Darragh: "He's out with friends."

I had been there for my boys, but not there; home, but not home. I wanted that to change. I didn't ever want them to feel like I didn't see them, hear them, or care for them.

A conversation with Marie drifted into my mind.

"What does responsibility mean to you?" Marie had asked me.

"I don't know, Marie."

"The ability to respond, Paddy. How are you going to respond right now with what I'm saying to you?" Marie looked me in the eye. She had a way of cutting right to my heart.

How *was* I going to respond to Darragh and Patrick and their need for a healthy, present dad who loved them with his whole heart?

Even worse, as I thought about what Darragh had said, I wondered. *If Darragh hadn't gone with me tonight, was it possible I would have gone to the pub, and not to Helen's?*

The question cut into me.

⟶◦ ◦⟵

During Christmas week, the donkey sanctuary sent me out on an emergency call to Baltimore, a small village in South Cork. A farmer had called, asking for help with a mother and newborn foal.

The farmer was a very old man with just one leg. We walked back to the little barn, a three-walled shed with one side open to the elements. In one corner was a jenny lying on the ground, but she wasn't moving. When I got closer, I could tell she wasn't breathing either. Next to her was a tiny little foal—weak, but very much alive.

A neighbor came by and told me the donkey had died two days before, right after giving birth, but he didn't want to tell the farmer. It was hard to tell what had happened to the jenny, but she must have hung on long enough to get her new foal out of the birth sac, cleaned up and dry. Baby donkeys look like little fluffy teddy bears when they are born; their extra-long coats help trap warm air and keep them cozy.

The foal, whom we named Tinsel, had been nursing from her mother for those two days, getting those first few important meals of mother's milk, including the immunity-boosting colostrum she needed. Outside it was wet and freezing cold, but as she snuggled up close to her mother's furry coat, Tinsel had been warm and dry enough, with just enough milk, to hang on until help arrived.

Tiny Tinsel stood up as we approached. She was a little wobbly, swaying back and forth on her long legs, but I could tell this two-day-old Christmas miracle baby was going to be tall and sleek someday with a beautiful, dark brown coat.

I picked her up and carried her out to the van lined with soft straw, then drove her back to the sanctuary where she was given a nice warm bottle of milk and put into a straw bed under a heat lamp to keep her warm. Tinsel was special, and we gave her lots of love and attention. This little one shouldn't have survived, but somehow life had come from death.

That first glimpse of Tinsel's bright little face, so very much alive, stayed with me like a new and fresh beacon of hope for my soul. It was a testament to nature and the God who created her. He had taken care of this little one and provided for her in the worst of circumstances.

If God cared for Tinsel and made a way for her to hold on and have a chance at living, was he doing the same for me? If he could make sure Tinsel had the help she needed at just the right time, wouldn't he continue to make sure I had help too? Finding Tinsel and bringing her back to the sanctuary gave me a strong and beautiful picture of rescue just when I needed it. If I could just hold on to that feeling of being seen for who I was that night in Cork City, cared for and loved despite my failures, I just might have a chance at a full recovery.

I still didn't have much money and the gifts weren't fancy that Christmas, but Darragh, Patrick, and I had a safe home with Mam and Dad, filled with love and laughter. On Christmas Eve Mam made her famous sausage stuffing to go with the turkey. Dad passed around sweets and biscuits and kept offering cups of strong tea. His motto is "It's not tea unless a mouse can run across it." The rest of the family came over—my sisters and their husbands and kids, and we went to Mass that night. I teased my sisters (whom I had taken to calling the three witches), they got mad at me, and all was right with the world.

I knew I wasn't going to wake up with a perfect life and my problems weren't going to all magically disappear. I still had PTSD, a mixed-up alcoholic brain, and a heart scarred by hurts. There was still plenty of work to do to make something of myself.

But I was sober, I had a job, I had my family, I had the donkeys, and now, it seemed I might have a future. It was the best Christmas gift ever.

That Christmas morning, my first one sober since I was a boy, I got up early and went to Mass with Mam. When we got home, she kept looking at me in amazement because I was usually in the pubs on Christmas Eve and hungover on Christmas morning.

"Mam, what can I do to help? Do you want me to put out the plates?"

"No, it's all done," she said, waving me off. I looked at the feast she had prepared—turkey and ham, Yorkshire puddings, brussels sprouts and turnips, mashed potatoes and gravy, and fresh baked soda bread. Off to the side was a big bowl of bread-and-butter pudding for dessert, along with some trifles. I inhaled the warm and rich scents of a mother's love, baked into her Christmas dinner. Had I ever told her how much I loved the food she made for us?

"Mam, I'm here. I want to help. What can I do?"

She smiled, her eyes twinkling and happy.

"How about a cup of tea, Mam?"

So I made us tea. Mam is a real tea sampler, tasting it with a small spoon to see if the tea is up to scratch, then adding milk in drips, and stirring until it is nice and milky, medium but not too strong, no sugar. We sat and talked and drank our tea. It was one of the best times I've ever spent with Mam.

Afterward I went over to the patio door and stepped outside. I looked toward the misty green hills, took a deep breath of the fresh, clean air, and let out a long, joyous donkey call. The donkeys at the sanctuary answered back, their voices ringing out with a sound better than any church bell. Tinsel couldn't bray yet, but I knew she was there, safe and warm with a belly full of warm milk.

"Oh, Patrick, will you just stop doing that?" Mam was laughing now, her face alight. "Will you ever stop it?"

CHAPTER FIFTEEN

NEW EYES AND NOLLAIG

✠

There is a window open from my heart to yours.

RUMI

JANUARY 6 IS A SPECIAL DAY celebrated in Ireland. *Nollaig na mBan,* meaning "little Christmas" or "women's Christmas,"[3] marks the end of the Christmas season. In Irish tradition, this day is when Irish men take on the household work for the day and women go out to enjoy themselves with friends. Just over a month after my second birthday in November, *Nollaig na mBan* came along, but I didn't have someone to share this special day with. At least not yet.

But I was walking around with what felt like new eyes and a new heart. When I first picked up the drink, I was a boy, and when I put it down, I went back to experiencing everything as a young boy again—the green grass, animals, and people, too.

My brand-new eyes had to learn how to refocus, to step out of

---

[3] In some religious traditions, it's also called The Feast of the Epiphany, celebrating the visit of the Magi to the newborn Jesus Christ.

the fog I had been trapped in and see clearly again. I had to refocus on good things, for myself and for my family.

The feeling reminded me of the apostle Paul's encounter with Jesus on the road to Damascus, where he saw a bright light and was blinded for three days because he saw the Lord in person. His sight was restored in Damascus, but the change was much, much bigger than that. Paul was a new man, changed forever by his face-to-face encounter with God.

From that day forward Paul became God's man, telling those he met about the Good News, and that a changed life is possible. This whole story felt real to me because I had been on that very road when I was in the army, but it felt even more real to me now because I had actually experienced it for myself.

For so many years I was like a tethered, blinkered donkey. These range animals were often tied to a rock or fence with short ropes or lines. Sometimes their feet were hobbled together, almost like shackles, so they couldn't walk and wander off.

While working, they were harnessed with complicated lines and straps, links and buckles across their backs, under their bellies, and around their heads, to keep them attached to work wagons and carts. Good owners made sure all of this was safe and comfortable, but not everyone paid attention to the donkeys' safety and welfare as closely as they could have.

To help them stay focused, blinkers, or blinders, were sometimes used on harnessed donkeys—leather shields to the side of their eyes, so they couldn't see behind them or to the side.

In a real sense, I was a donkey who had been blinkered, hobbled, and tethered but was still trying to strain ahead and pull a heavy load under a painful harness. When I was born again that night in the room with Marie and my group and given new eyes and a new heart, I was set free from it all.

Not only was all that pain an unbearable weight that I'd been under for most of my life, but I visualized the mark of the cross on my back, just like a donkey's.

⊹⇥═◉ ◉═⇤⊹

Nollaig was not only the name of a Christmas tradition—it was also the name of a donkey I helped rescue during the Christmas season. We got a call from a farm in a nearby town, only five miles from the sanctuary. It was a cold, wet day, and I found Nollaig shivering in a field all by himself.

His coat was patchy, and on closer inspection, I saw he was covered in scabs where clumps of hair had peeled off, leaving bare spots. Sometimes birds attack these raw spots, pecking at them and causing further damage. I gently ran my hand over his coat, and even the areas where he still had hair were lumpy, meaning there were hidden problems underneath. He must have been very uncomfortable, and I knew in his condition he wouldn't be able to keep warm in an Irish December. His feet were in an appalling state as well, with overgrown hooves and what appeared to be a fungal infection that had started to rot them from underneath.

How had Nollaig gotten into this state? He was a sweet donkey and didn't deserve this kind of neglect. I soon got my answer. His owner was an alcoholic, and his state of mind was clear as I looked around at the neglected fields, sheds, and house. Everything was dirty and falling apart, on a steep decline just like the man.

Nollaig came with us to the sanctuary, and with medical treatment, help for his hooves from the farrier, good food, and a warm and dry place to sleep at night, he recovered. But it took some time. Once his skin and coat recovered, he showed his true colors—a rich brown and white.

It's never easy to see an animal in this kind of condition, but it's even worse when it's preventable. Being one month sober, I wasn't out of the woods and was really only at the start of my recovery, but the story of Nollaig sent a strong message to me about the consequences of yielding to temptation. The farmer's choice to live his life this way had a strong impact on Nollaig, and he just barely escaped death. Did the farmer care about this little one? I can't say, but the memory of how Nollaig looked that day is with me still.

Nollaig was lucky he got help in time, but not all donkeys are as lucky. Sometimes a donkey is so sick or has been neglected for so long, the animal can't be saved and has to be humanely put down.

I had to assist with this at times, and while it is mostly painless for the animal, it can be frightening. I would try to help usher each donkey through this transition, and over time I began to understand what was most comforting.

Standing close to the donkey's side, I'd put my right arm over and around the neck, with my right hand curving up past his ears and over his eyes so he couldn't see what was happening. The vet would have an injection prepared, and I didn't want the donkey to see the syringe or the vet's face.

I'd stroke the donkey's neck with my left hand, leaning into his shoulder and talking quietly to him.

"It's okay. Everything's going to be alright," I'd say over and over in a gentle murmur.

I wanted each donkey to feel loved and cared for. I pray they did, and in these sacred moments they knew we tried to help the best we could.

Within thirty seconds or so after the drug entered his bloodstream, the donkey's legs would relax and begin to buckle. I'd hold tight around his neck and slowly help him to the ground, where he could lie down.

I'd sit and gently stroke him, until his final breath. It was a peaceful end, and I hoped this beautiful creature would feel loved and cared for in his last moments. No one, including a donkey, deserves to be thrown away or to die alone.

This final goodbye was never an easy one, but the further into recovery I got, and the healthier my soul grew, the more I saw it as a sacred act of ushering a precious life from this planet to a better place . . . hopefully with plenty of sweet green grass and sunshine.

As strange as it sounds, Marie had done this for me that night in Cork. I was a dying man, my life draining away one glass at a time, and she took a hold on my neck and with a strong but loving grip, ushered me into a new one. The old me needed to be put to rest, so that the real me locked inside could come out and live and breathe and see all of the beauty and wonder of the world again. My eyes, and my soul, had been wiped clean. How could I ever repay her?

One way was to take this new path seriously and work hard to keep going. I am part of a support group that has become a very important part of my journey.

I resolved to take better care of myself, and so I joined a hill walking club in the village that went on regular hikes around the countryside, including climbing some of our mountains.

I started a new morning ritual that I've continued to this day. I wake up early, get dressed, go downstairs, and get a fire going in the kitchen fireplace. I have a large framed picture of Jesus, and I take that out and lean it up against the brick hearth. Then I kneel down on the wood floor and pray. The prayers are familiar—I say the St. Francis prayer, the Rosary, and the Lord's Prayer.

Lord, make me an instrument of your peace:
where there is hatred, let me sow love;
where there is injury, pardon;
where there is doubt, faith;
where there is despair, hope;

where there is darkness, light;
where there is sadness, joy.
O divine Master, grant that I may not so much seek
to be consoled as to console,
to be understood as to understand,
to be loved as to love.
For it is in giving that we receive,
it is in pardoning that we are pardoned,
and it is in dying that we are born to eternal life.
Amen.

I also say the Rosary, along with the Lord's Prayer:

Our Father which art in heaven, Hallowed be thy name.
Thy kingdom come. Thy will be done on earth, as it is in
heaven. Give us this day our daily bread. And forgive us
our trespasses, as we forgive them that trespass against us.
And lead us not into temptation, but deliver us from evil:
For thine is the kingdom, and the power, and the glory,
for ever and ever. Amen.[4]

There is something very powerful about this simple ritual that
sets me straight. I say these prayers and others, handing my will
and my life over to God for that day.

Next I lie down on my back on the wood floor and breathe
for a minute, sometimes listening to quiet music. I talk to God
like he's sitting right there in the kitchen, having a cup of tea at
the table, with me on the floor at his feet. Sometimes I use words,
and sometimes I just give him my feelings, my worries, and my
fears. All of it.

---

4 Jesus' prayer in Matthew 6:9-13.

After that, I listen. Some people call it meditation, but I want to hear what God has to say to me, and this is the only time of the day it's quiet enough.

Sometimes my thoughts wander, going from worrying about my problems or what's going on at my job or in my family to what's happening on a global level. Sometimes my conversations with God are random—expressing stray thoughts and feelings, reliving memories and images.

This time with the Lord Jesus has become very important to me. For so many years, Jesus was just a word on a page or part of a prayer at church. The God I thought of when I was growing up seemed like a God of fear to me.

But I see him differently now. He's alive in me and he transformed me from a man bent on self-destruction to a man who wants to live in God's light. This wild donkey of a man has been saved and redeemed from death and despair. I know I wouldn't be alive without divine intervention, and through the help of a nun named Marie and many other people who loved me and cared for me.

It's a little embarrassing because we usually don't talk like this in Ireland, but this is who I am today. This is about the spiritual side of my being, this is how I freely talk to my family, and this is what I do to stay alive. I want to say what is true, because for so long I lived a life that wasn't true.

Here's the truest truth of my life—the more I depend on God, the more independent I am in my life from the beliefs and the habits that were so harmful to me. The more I love and serve him, the more free I am. In forgetting myself, I have found myself.

It's all a great mystery, so it is.

My morning ritual of connecting to God is what keeps me alive. Every day is a struggle, and if I want to live, I must pray. So I choose life.

This time with God also reminds me that my life isn't just about me. For so long, before my transformation, I'd only thought about myself and my problems and what I wanted. I hadn't made room for anyone or anything else in my heart. Now, with this daily practice, I'm reminded that I'm not the center of my life anymore.

⋄⊱─◉ ◉─⊰⋄

There's a story in the Gospel of Mark about Jesus healing a blind man. The sightless man's friends brought him to Jesus and begged for healing. Jesus took him by the hand, led him outside the village, spit on the man's eyes, and laid his hands on him.

"Do you see anything?" Jesus asked the man.

"I see people; they look like trees walking around."

Jesus put his hands on the man's eyes again. Then his eyes were opened, his sight was restored, and he saw everything clearly.[5]

I love this story for so many reasons—Jesus responded when the blind man's friends asked for help. The blind man couldn't seem to do this on his own—he needed his herd to intervene. Jesus took him outside the village to be alone. Then Jesus touched him and healed him, but it wasn't instantaneous. It took two tries! Healing for this man was a process. It also took me two tries to put away the drink and find healing. Jesus didn't seem to see the healing of the blind man as a failure; it was just the manner of this particular healing. Maybe some of us with darkened eyes and hearts need the touch of the Lord more than once.

When I finished work at the sanctuary each day, I'd walk up the hill and stay there to watch the sunset color the sky. It was as if I were seeing it for the first time in my life. *How long have I been away from all this? How have I never looked up?*

---

5 Mark 8:22-25, NIV

It was like the honeymoon period of a new friendship or a love relationship. Sometimes I felt like I was walking on air or I was surrounded by a golden glow of sunbeams. The world was beautiful—how had I not noticed?

My first few months of sobriety, I would climb up onto the big round bales of hay by the barn and look out over the landscape to the Kerry Mountains. I'd lie down, resting on the hay as it got dark, listening to the birds singing. Sometimes Darragh, who was eight at the time, came with me, and we'd lie there together and listen to the donkeys feeding. It was like an evening meditation— hundreds of donkeys lined up, heads down, chewing their hay together. They seemed to go into a meditative state, too, and an evening peace settled over the sanctuary as the day turned to dusk.

These moments gave me a sense of serenity, something I don't think I'd ever felt before. I was transformed—seeing and hearing and sensing things as if I were a new person. The shadow me was starting to melt away, and through my brokenness and surren- der, the light was creeping in through the cracks—just like Marie said—and clearing out the darkness.

I was thirty-three years old, the same age as our Lord when he rose from the grave with his new body and new eyes. And now, like the donkeys, I knew for certain I bore the imprint of his cross on my back.

CHAPTER SIXTEEN

the girl below
the hill

People live in each other's shelter.

IRISH PROVERB

What we find in a soul mate is not something wild to tame,
but something wild to run with.

ROBERT BRAULT

About a year into my recovery, I met someone else who prayed. Her name was Eileen, and she was the beautiful girl in the village who gave me my first kiss before we took such different paths.

Eileen had grown up in a traditional Irish cottage, not far from my house, where her mother reigned over the cozy kitchen and baked Irish scones by the dozen for anyone who wanted to stop by for a mug of tea. Eileen's mam and dad were like mine—they had big hearts and took in whatever creature, whether human or animal, that needed a warm place to shelter and be fed. They had five girls (Eileen was in the middle) and one boy, and so the house was full of love and laughter.

Eileen was a smart and serious-minded girl—I called her group of friends the nerd herd. I knew she had gone to university in Cork City to study arts and then trained to be a primary school teacher.

Later Eileen earned a master's degree in child and adolescent therapy, with a specialty in play therapy. She'd started a counseling business and built a beautiful two-story house for herself and her son, also named Daragh, next to the cottage where she grew up. In 2018 she became principal of the village school, the same one I had once run away from, never to return.

Even though our village was small and our paths sometimes crossed, I felt like I hadn't seen her—*really* seen her—in years, until one fateful day at the Donkey Sanctuary.

I was there for a fundraiser with my Darragh and little Patrick. When Eileen walked up, I felt a shock go through me, like I was seeing her for the very first time, and her green eyes seemed to look right through me.

EILEEN

When I saw Patrick at the Donkey Sanctuary fundraiser, a flood of childhood memories came back. I vividly remember the day he ran out of the classroom. School days weren't quite as interesting after he left, although I didn't miss his dog barks or donkey calls. He was part of the neighborhood gang of children who played tennis on our lawn and hung out behind my family's cottage. We were both quiet, though, and nearly invisible to each other.

After he was sent to another school, the only time I saw him was at set dancing class every week at The Old Walls. Set dancing is similar to American square dancing. We learned choreography to different couples' dances and were often paired with the boys. One night, Patrick's friend Barry arranged for us to kiss after dance class.

I was nervous all through class and didn't say a word to Patrick; I just watched him out of the corner of my eye. I'm sure he was doing the same to me. When class was over, I went outside to the prearranged spot in the corner, and he kissed me. Or I kissed him. Actually, we kissed each other, and there were a lot of teeth involved. I don't think there were many, if any, words exchanged.

A week later we kissed again, and that was the end of it.

Years later, when we'd occasionally run into each other in the pub we would mock each other about our first kiss.

"Hey, Paddy Piranha!"

"What's the *craic*, Barracuda Mouth?"

I'd sometimes hear a story about his pranks or drunken escapades, but since he never showed me much attention when we were in the same room, I mostly forgot about him.

Now, here we were at the Donkey Sanctuary, standing face-to-face near the horse-and-cart rides. I had seen Patrick holding his two boys and I made my way with Daragh through the crowd to greet him.

"Patrick Barrett. How nice to see you."

"Eileen! You're looking well. And who is the handsome young man with you?"

"This is my son, Daragh."

"Are you going to do the treasure hunt next?" my Daragh asked Patrick.

"No, not right now," Patrick said with a smile.

"Why not, Dad? Is it because you have your two treasures already in your arms?" Patrick's Darragh piped up.

I laughed at this eight-year-old's sweet observation and smiled in my soul. *He already has his treasures.*

PATRICK

Seeing Eileen again awakened something inside me. I'd always had an attraction to her, but I could never pin down the feeling or understand it until the drink was out of my life. I had felt like I wasn't good enough for her and ashamed of what I had become. *What would she want to do with me?*

Whenever I had seen her around the village, her strength and goodness seemed to overwhelm me. Every time I'd felt so small and like I wanted to run away, but instead acted like I didn't see her or didn't care. But this time was different.

At the time I was actually living with Eileen's only brother, Sean, who felt sorry for me, I think. We'd been friends since our school days and always had a lot in common with so many sisters to contend with. After seeing Eileen at the fundraiser, and as New Year's Eve approached, Sean asked Eileen if he could invite me to the small party she was hosting.

I wasn't sure if I should go, but Mam gave me a push. "Will you ever go down for a bit of dinner?" she said. "I'll mind the boys. You're okay—don't have a drink. You're doing great."

So I said yes. I'll come.

EILEEN

When Sean asked if he could invite Patrick to the party, I said, "Yes, of course!" I didn't like the thought of him being all alone at the start of a new year.

That night Patrick was the first guest to arrive. He was wearing a gorgeous navy jumper and looked so handsome. He greeted Daragh, who was playing *Call of Duty* on the PlayStation in the front room.

After I hung up Patrick's coat, I led him into the kitchen and asked, "Can you hop onto the worktop to put up my Christmas lights?" I wanted them along the tops of the cabinets to light up the ceiling.

"Of course!" he said, a little nervously.

While he worked on the lights, I checked on the brie heating in the oven and finished prepping the chicken and mushroom *vol-au-vent*. I kept looking at him while he worked. He seemed so happy and content in himself.

This isn't the Patrick Barrett I remember.

After dinner he loaded up the dishwasher, and after I turned it on, the heavy load combined with the fact that it wasn't permanently attached made it start vibrating its way out and into the kitchen. It was about to run me down when Patrick dived onto the floor to block the dishwasher and save my ankles. It felt nice to have someone watch out for me.

Afterward, we sat on the couch while he told me about his counseling course and asked about my work with children. It was the very first time I'd ever had a proper conversation with him.

PATRICK

We had a good laugh about the near miss with the dishwasher, Sean joking that I saved Eileen, but it felt good. I came away feeling some kind of connection with her, along with a feeling of wanting to mind her—take care of her—that never went away.

EILEEN

Patrick had joined my hill walking club, called the Mountain Goat Ramblers, right before we went on a day trip to the Ballyhoura Mountains. To be honest, I wasn't looking forward to walking alongside him—even though we'd had a fun evening at my New Year's celebration, I didn't think we had much in common.

There were about twenty of us and we met at the trail park. It was cold and raining hard—not the best conditions for a walk or a conversation. But we ended up walking in step on the descent and Patrick began to tell me about his recovery, his boys, how he had found God in his life, and how content he had begun to feel. Before I knew it, tears were streaming down my face. *He really has changed.* I could see and hear the difference, and I was genuinely happy for him and his boys. It was nice having a new friend in the village.

PATRICK

I couldn't believe I would be spending the whole day with Eileen, even in the freezing rain. Everything inside of me yearned to be with her, even if it was just a walk with a crowd of other people. I had so much I wanted to say, but we got separated on the way up the mountain, and one thing or another kept us apart. Once everyone was at the summit, we gathered in the ruins of a shepherd's stone hut. The roofless shelter offered little protection from the cold and rain; we call it *muggy* weather. I was chilled to the bone and hungry. As I opened up my gourmet lunch—a can of Batchelor's Beans—I heard a familiar laugh.

"How do you eat that?" Eileen asked, a bit of a sparkle in her eyes.

"Mmmmm," I said, through a mouthful of cold beans. "Would you like some?"

I made sure we were together on the way down the mountain. As we walked beside each other, I opened up and shared some of my life's struggles with her, and she really listened. I wasn't running away or running into a pub anymore. I was walking with someone who was paying attention to what I was saying. Quiet, honest conversations were new to me, and I didn't quite know how to do them. I wasn't used to showing someone who I really was.

When she started to cry, I was at a loss for words.

Later that night, I texted her: *I'm sorry I made you cry.*

EILEEN

Listening to Patrick tell me the story of his recovery, and how he had found God and was beginning to feel content, touched my soul. Before I realized it, tears began streaming down my face.

I began to look forward to his messages after that, but I didn't have any romantic thoughts. Then I went to a meditation day with his sister Helen, where we put together vision boards to set our intentions for the coming year. I deliberately didn't include anything based on romance or marriage, because I already felt happy and content.

After we were done, I checked my phone and had a text from Patrick. In the car Helen teased me about him. "He would be lovely for you!"

I'd just begun to laugh at her comment when, in a strange coincidence, he literally drove right past us.

PATRICK

A week later, I was getting the house ready for a visit from Eileen. I had invited her for tea.

On my page-a-day desk calendar was a Gandhi quote: "Happiness is when what you think, what you say, and what you do are in harmony."

That's what I want to be for Eileen—a whole man whose mind, body, soul, and heart are aligned, open, and honest.

I pulled the page off the calendar and put it in my wallet. I wanted her to see the real me, the true me, and the vulnerable me. No bravado to impress her, just a genuine and honest connection. I knew Eileen would be in my life forevermore.

My strategy was for us to watch a movie and then keep her at the house as long as possible by making her copious amounts of tea. I was a little nervous, like that lad at The Old Walls, but it was a healthy nervousness. I had a good feeling about this. And I wanted another kiss.

EILEEN

When Patrick called and asked if I'd come over for tea, I accepted, but after I said yes I had second thoughts. *Was this a date?*

I knew he was attracted to me, but I felt comfortable with myself and where I was, and I wasn't particularly looking for anyone. I was okay with being friends.

I decided I'd go to his house for tea and give him the "I just want to be friends" talk. But it didn't happen that way. Instead, we fell into powerful, deep conversations about everything—love, life, and God. It felt like a divine moment where we spoke from our hearts. Then, we both fell silent and a powerful Presence entered the room. I could literally feel a channel of absolute light connecting my soul to Patrick's.

I don't know how long the moment lasted, but I didn't want it to stop.

PATRICK

I believed God was dwelling inside of me and inside of Eileen, and when we were together that night the presence of God filled the room. No judgment, no shame, no baggage attached to it, just a moment of pure, serene love.

It was the same strange electric feeling in my heart that I felt as a child looking deep into the eyes of Aran, and later Nollaig, Jerusalem, Tinsel, and Jacksie. I saw it in the eyes of my newborn babies, and in the eyes of Marie. It was pure love.

What made this sense of love even more powerful was the peace that came with it. When we stopped talking, the feeling became stronger in the silence.

"Are you feeling it?" Eileen finally asked.

"Yes, there's a real presence in the room."

To this day, I treasure and keep that experience close in my heart, not knowing if it will ever be duplicated again.

I knew Eileen was a churchgoer, but I'd never before realized how deep her faith and spirituality went and how connected to God she was. I believe I was attracted to her as a woman and also attracted to the presence of God in her. My spiritual journey had led me to her, someone who had been there in the village all along. Why hadn't I seen her this way before?

EILEEN

About a week later, Patrick asked me to come over and watch a movie with him. This time I knew it was a date, but he sat on one end of the couch and I sat on the other. I was waiting for him to make a move. At one point, he tried to show me a magic trick using a cross necklace he wore, but he messed it up, got embarrassed, and slinked back to his end of the couch.

When the movie was over, I got up to leave.

"Would you like a cup of tea before you go?" he asked.

"That would be lovely."

After about five or six cups of tea, I went to the door, where he gave me a hug, then kissed me. It was electric, and I knew my life, my heart, and my soul would never be the same again—I was finally home. From that night on, our love blossomed. I was so proud of how hard he was working to make a new life for himself—and now for us.

PATRICK

One day I got an urgent call from Eileen. A hedgehog had gotten trapped inside her garage and needed to be rescued. When I arrived, I put on gloves and carefully picked up the creature, which had tucked itself into a small, spiny ball. I dripped a few drops of water onto its middle (a trick I learned from my grandmother), and the hedgehog started moving, opening up like a beautiful rose going into bloom, emerging into the light.

I wasn't a hedgehog whisperer, but I took it home to feed it and the hedgehog learned to trust me. A few days later, he was strong and healthy enough to be released back into his hedge.

My new love with Eileen reminded me of the hedgehog. I was learning to open up and trust another human being, and to give love and accept it too.

EILEEN

On the twenty-eighth of February 2014, Patrick told me he loved me and I melted. My heart and soul were knit to his. We exchanged boxes of love letters and loads of texts, and he got down on his knee and proposed in the same corner outside The Old Walls where we shared our first kiss. It wasn't quite like the movies; the pigeons were startled and flying off the roof, and it was so dark I couldn't see the ring. But I floated through the next day, and I knew Patrick was my soulmate.

PATRICK

This may sound totally mad, but I really believe when I first said *I love you* to Eileen, they weren't my own words. I felt compelled to tell her I love her. I remember hugging her, and it was the weirdest feeling. It was like she melted into me.

It wasn't long after that we started talking about getting married, and we got engaged in March. I was too frightened to ask her father for her hand in marriage, afraid he wouldn't give his consent because he might think of me as the old Patrick. Today I hope he sees that I love her, take care of her, and will always be there for her.

Eileen and I stood outside The Old Walls in the dark, and when I got down on one knee, she couldn't see me.

"What are you doing?" she asked.

"Look, I thought this would be the appropriate place." We started laughing, and just then a pigeon—our only witness—nesting in the roof above us started cooing loudly.

EILEEN

When I was about five or six, Mom was putting me to bed one night and I told her my heart felt full up with God's love, like a gold cup with all of the gold spilling out of it.

I always felt a close connection to God, even as a small girl. I spent a lot of time out in the garden and the fields but never felt alone; I always felt a Presence near me. I could spend hours making a daisy chain and feeling such contentment in my soul. I began to journal when I was eleven years old, and that became my way of praying; God always answers me in the pages.

Growing up as a Catholic in Ireland, there was a lot of Catholic guilt and an emphasis on your "wrongness"—that you're a bad person and that faith equals suffering. It wasn't until my late twenties that I was reintroduced to a God who loves us unconditionally, his love flowing into us and through us like liquid gold. God wants joy and happiness and love for us, not suffering and strife. Knowing God like this, I felt like that young girl again, my soul alight with the love I had found. There were no conditions on knowing God's love.

Seeing Patrick filling up with this love drew me to him, and I felt like we connected on that level. The day of our wedding, I floated through it knowing Patrick was my soulmate, with nothing bigger than this truth.

PATRICK

Ten months later, we got married on a beautiful New Year's Day at Liscarroll Church with all of our family and friends together with us. Dad, Darragh, little Patrick, and I rode from the donkey sanctuary to the church in a cart pulled by a donkey.

One of my brothers-in-law, Mick, had refurbished the old donkey cart and it was covered in flowers and ferns from the woods. I had paid a visit to the Travellers to ask to borrow a donkey trained to the cart and came away with a jack—an intact male—trained for racing. Not ideal for pulling a wedding cart but he was the only cart donkey I could find, and he was a beautiful shiny black.

It was a quiet morning since anyone who wasn't going to the wedding was probably sleeping in from staying up late the night before to celebrate the arrival of 2015. It was quiet, that is, except for one ambitious lorry driver rumbling down through the main street of Liscarroll.

The giant articulated lorry was too big for the narrow street, but he came on anyway, spooking the donkey. Terrified, the donkey started jumping in fear, catching his leg on the cart, and then started backing up in reverse through the village with me and Dad both trying to calm him down. We nearly crashed into three or four cars with the cart, and it almost became a donkey race, after all.

As soon as the lorry disappeared into the distance, the donkey began to relax and pulled us up to the church, where we finally landed safe and sound.

Eileen walked up the aisle with her father while her Daragh sang "The Book of Love." I looked at her in her beautiful white dress, and I was overwhelmed with her beauty. She was radiant.

Then our eyes met. *I can't believe I'm marrying the girl who gave me my first kiss.* Those feelings of shyness and nervousness came right back. When she got to the front of the church, it was my turn to kiss her, this time in front of our families and the village.

After the wedding, we went up to the top of the hill at the donkey sanctuary and took our photos—Eileen standing up on the rock and leaning down to kiss me. The winds blew as they always did and lifted her veil up toward the heavens, with the fields flowing away from us, the village and the castle in the background, and the green hills like a vibrant emerald embrace. The donkeys gathered around and watched it all, curious and watchful, their shiny black eyes taking it all in.

So much had happened in my life up there, and now Eileen, my *anam cara*, was there with me too.

EILEEN

We probably were a little naive. I was consumed with my love for Patrick, but I knew little of the struggles of alcoholism and I brought some of my own fears along with me too. But we belonged together and our love for each other never wavered. I've never allowed a human being to see me and know me as deeply as Patrick, and now along with his Darragh and little Patrick, I am one of his treasures too. And so is my Daragh!

One night we were having a cup of tea when Patrick told me about the night on the hill at the sanctuary when he cried out to God in desperation. Something clicked in my memory.

On a November night I had taken a walk down through the village and past the castle with my little dog Cleo. I was lonely, yearning for someone to love and to love me. I wanted someone to share my life with, who would treasure me and Daragh forever. I also wanted someone to sit and have tea with after work while we both talked about our day.

There were no streetlights down by the donkey sanctuary and the stars were so strong and bright that night, against the rich, velvety black sky. I sat down on the stone wall opposite the hill, with Cleo at my feet. The air was so cold I could see my breath. I stared at three stars that shone more brightly than the others, and they almost seemed as if they were dancing around each other in the sky, but gently, slowly, softly.

God was there with me, and I handed my loneliness, my fears, and my desire for a partner over to him. I felt a surge of love flow through me and a certainty that God was taking care of me and my future soulmate. I had a strong feeling that my husband was somewhere not too far away, and that he was on his way to me.

Then, I knew it was true. I had been there! "Patrick, I was at the bottom of the hill, only ten meters away from you!"

If anyone had ever told me I would end up with Patrick Barrett, the boy I hated when I was thirteen, I would have laughed. But I believe in faith, not coincidences. God is at the center of our love, and he always will be. He has to be, because I've seen Patrick in his pain and his torture, and I am so proud that he has fought such battles to become the man he is today.

We have held each other through everything, and I know we will until the day we leave this earth. Until then, you can find us having our chats over cups of tea in the kitchen.

There was a time I hated Patrick Barrett, but not anymore.

This Patrick is the one I love.

PATRICK

I have three Eileens in my life: my mam, my sister, and now my wife. The name *Eileen* is a Gaelic name and means "bright, shining one."

That she is.

CHAPTER SEVENTEEN

JACKSIE'S SONG

✦

You make springs pour water into the ravines,
so streams gush down from the mountains. . . .
And the wild donkeys quench their thirst.

PSALM 104:10-11, NLT

REMEMBER JACKSIE, the abandoned foal at the beginning of my story? He's such a big and important part of my life. He came into the sanctuary as a newborn when I was a newborn, too, with my sobriety and my faith. We were babies together, so we were.

His first interaction with the world was through humans—my family and me and some of the hardworking people at the Donkey Sanctuary—as we fed him every three hours and kept him cuddled up and warm in the stable under the heat lamp until he was old enough to join the others.

He'd be so excited when I came at night to feed him, wagging his tail like a puppy and nodding his head up and down. Sometimes he'd try to wrap his neck or even leg around me in his version of a donkey hug. I would bray to him and nicker over him, trying to sound like his mother. He listened to me so carefully and looked into my eyes with his small shiny black ones peeping out of his fluffy brown and white coat. Some nights I'd fall asleep on the straw next to him, warmed by this big fluffy teddy bear with much longer ears.

Jacksie soaked up all the attention and began to look at me and try to imitate my facial expressions, like a human baby. When donkeys feel comfortable and safe with you, they'll show you a thousand different facial expressions, but you have to watch closely because they come and go incredibly fast. Donkeys can frown and look worried, show anger or irritation, express fear, act surprised or curious, and even smile and laugh.

Their lips are fuzzy and rubbery, and they can stretch them out, lift them up to show their teeth, twist them around in different directions, and use them almost like fingers to grab and pick up things to eat or to play with, like balls, brooms, or old rubber boots. The donkeys at the sanctuary love to pull the plastic ID collars off of each other and run away with them or slap each other with the ends. Donkeys can open doors and pick locks, which was true of my childhood friend, Aran. They love to pinch or nibble at you, like they do with each other when playing or showing affection.

Jacksie loved to nibble on me when he was young, and as he's gotten older, he likes to play bite. Donkeys are certainly cute but they can bite hard, so a play session with Jacksie often means I wrap one arm around his neck or head and grab the bottom of his jaw with my other hand to try to keep his lips from grabbing me and his teeth from taking a chunk out of me. I know he enjoys every minute of his mischievousness—his tail swishes back and forth in sheer delight.

He also likes to wrestle with me. When he was tiny, it was adorable to have him lie across my lap while I bottle-fed him, but it isn't quite as cute now when he is several hundred pounds of muscle and sinew. Adolescent donkeys get rougher when they play fight, standing up on their hind legs and boxing each other like kangaroos, pawing and biting. They can wrap their legs and necks around each other, like a wrestling hold, for more intense play. It looks vicious, but it's usually in good fun. However, humans aren't equipped for this level of roughhousing, and it has taken Jacksie some time to learn his limits with me and with the others who care for him now.

When I walk in the fields, Jacksie chases me, starts to jump, and wants to wrestle. Sometimes, when I rebuff him, he gets angry, turns his back on me, and sulks, giving me the cold shoulder for a while. He lays his ears back against his head and walks away in a bit of a huff.

Jacksie seems to genuinely care about me, and when he hears my voice, no matter where he is in the fields, he starts whining and crying in his donkey way, calling me to come over and be with him. He pretty much ignores everyone else. I'm not quite sure why he chose me as his favorite, but to this very day I think I still am.

He came into the sanctuary at a time when he needed me and I needed him, when I was fresh into recovery and starting my college work to become a counselor. He was my bridge back to working with the donkeys and returning to a kind of innocence. I consider him my jester who made me laugh when I really needed that too. Although he's a different species from me, he's closer than a friend—he's more like a brother.

Donkeys are very sensitive creatures with long memories, but they don't judge you for your troubles, and once they accept you in as a part of their herd, you feel a strong sense of belonging. That sense of belonging was part of finding myself again. It makes me crazy to think that people would beat a creature like Jacksie in anger, take a stick to his back, or let him lie in a field all alone, sick and in pain. Donkeys can feel pain. They understand when someone cares about them (or doesn't), and if they don't trust you or the situation, they might not show you their feelings, but those feelings are there inside of them. This I know.

Jacksie is like a family member, but I have my own human herd now. My marriage to Eileen made all of my dreams come true. I still can't believe she said yes!

Eileen's Daragh recently graduated from secondary school and is about to embark on a musical theatre course in the UK. Big Daragh graciously trusted me and welcomed me into his home. It was not an easy transition for him, I'm sure, but I'm in awe of what a compassionate young lad he is, multi-talented, and overall a well-rounded human being who makes the world a better place.

I'm also so proud to call myself Darragh and Patrick's father. They are such caring, compassionate, and resilient young men. What stands out most to me is how respectful they are of others. Darragh wants to be a soldier or a researcher working on a cure for cancer. Patrick wants to be a professional rugby player and a farmer, and he's caring for a flock of chickens at the moment. Eileen and I have two children together now, Ellen-Rose, almost four years old, and little Odhrán (*Oren*), two years old. Both are beautiful and smart like Eileen, thank God.

Our daughter Ellen-Rose was my first girl, and when she was born, I got to hold her first. She had light blue eyes and very fair skin, and I stared at her in shock and awe for many minutes. She was quiet and so full of light, and I laid her down on Eileen's chest where she snuggled up like a little lamb.

Baby Odhrán gave us a scare when he was born, though. My memories of Darragh's and Patrick's births are still with me, and so when our youngest was born and had trouble breathing, I was in a state. They kept him at the hospital in Cork City, and when he wasn't getting better after a week, they immediately transferred him by ambulance to Crumlin Hospital in Dublin. He was covered in wires and hooked up to so much equipment we couldn't ride with him and had to drive separately, a horrific journey.

Right after we arrived in Dublin, Eileen fell ill and was hospitalized on the other side of the city with a serious medical issue related to a birth complication that required surgery. I was so frightened of losing either of them. Family trauma like this was not new to me, but my response was. Since I didn't have time to go pray for Odhrán at the church in Mallow with Eileen so sick, too, I leaned on family and friends to pray for us and help us make it through. And they did.

The village was there for us during these health struggles. Everyone turned up at the church for a special Mass to pray for Odhrán's recovery, and knowing our friends and neighbors were thinking of us and praying for us meant so much. For that I am ever grateful.

Eileen's beautiful family, and her Daragh, held down the fort for us during those months, taking care of little Ellen-Rose when we needed to be with Odhrán. We were gone for nearly three months.

Now I have five treasures in my house (six, if you count Eileen), and I thank God every day during my prayers for saving me for these days. Our lives are full and even when life has its ups and downs like a roller-coaster ride, we're a family and we are doing life together. I'm in it for the long haul.

I remember a moment when my three sisters visited me in Dublin during the crisis with Odhrán. I was staying in special accommodations for parents of children in hospital, and my room was in a ward called Nazareth. I hadn't been with all my sisters for quite a while, and it was a welcome respite from the worry. There was laughter and joking amidst the tears as I honestly expressed my feelings and concerns. They weren't used to this kind of openness from me, and they got an inside peek at me and my life and who I had become, maybe for the very first time.

My behavior and attitude, marred by my drinking, had distanced us, and our time together during this stressful period for my family began to heal my relationship with them. I knew I had disappointed Debbie, Helen, and Eileen deeply, especially when Dad was sick. They'd been angry with me, and rightfully so, and Dad's brush with death bonded us together again. The four of us have vowed to take care of our parents as they get older and to make sure we're taking care of each other, too.

It's strange how even though I grew up in a big family with strong connections, I still often felt alone and disconnected. I was a lost soul, but I was finally finding my way back. My PTSD, my addictions, and the consequences of my life choices had dulled my memories of what it was like to be a part of the village and live close to the land and the animals. Jacksie has helped me to remember and reconnect with the best parts of my growing up there.

But the village of Liscarroll was struggling, along with many other small villages, to compete with newer stores and businesses in larger nearby cities where jobs were available. The Irish economy had taken a huge hit with the economic downturn of 2008 and unemployment was high. And even though the village had gotten smaller since I'd gone into the army, the sanctuary had expanded. More donkeys returned to the sanctuary from their temporary foster homes during the 2008 economic crisis and the need was great.

Addiction is selfish in nature—when I was in the throes of alcoholism, it's as if my eyes were permanently rolled inward, fretting over myself and my worries and desires. I didn't know how to unselfishly care for others, and so taking care of the donkeys, especially Jacksie, helped teach me how to care for others. My job at the sanctuary took me out of my own head so I could begin to learn how to have a generous, honest, and loving relationship with others. If it hadn't been for the donkeys, would I have been able to have the relationships I have now? I don't know. But I do know I would love to use what I've learned from the donkeys to help others, especially those with PTSD. God has planted a dream and a hope within me to help others the way I've been helped, and maybe someday to open a therapy center where donkeys can be part of the healing process. Their acceptance, friendship, intelligence, and sense of humor is good medicine.

Through my educational experience, I've learned that I was born with a high degree of empathy and can feel what is happening inside of others. When I was a boy, I didn't know how to handle this sensitivity or create boundaries to keep myself from feeling too much. Research is showing that people like me might have hyperactive mirror neuron systems in our neurological wiring, meaning our brains feel the pain of others to a very high degree.

This kind of nervous system can react in a stronger way to external stimuli, including stress of all kinds, and managing this overload on the senses is not always easy to understand or to carry out. But it's crucial to learn how to be empathetic and caring toward others without taking on their feelings or carrying their pain. Boys, especially, are told to be tough and act like men, so they can feel like there's something wrong with them, or that they don't fit in.

I remember the very first day when I showed up at the front gate of the army barracks and was sternly ordered: "Leave your feelings at the gate." I took it to heart and visualized leaving my feelings there as I put on my uniform. I was no longer myself; I'd become property of the military.

That profound act of putting on a uniform became a Jekyll and Hyde act with me, as I learned to put on different personalities or personas in different situations. As time went on and the darkness grew inside of me, I found it harder and harder to switch out of that dark side. And sometimes, even today, that switch happens quickly and without warning in quick flashes of anger that make no sense. Is it because of alcoholism and the change in my internal wiring at such a young age? Or PTSD? Or a combination of the two? I don't know, but it happens to me even without a drink in me.

With PTSD, repeated trauma can cause what some consider to be almost like an injury, causing a state of fight-or-flight that becomes habitual and hard to escape or shut down. For me, I would go into an unexpected rage, especially after drinking, and I'm told my eyes would go black and my face pale. I've had episodes where I've thrown objects around and broken up a room. Then I'd fall asleep, wake up the next day, and have no idea what had happened. It was a walking blackout, punctuated with rage, and further stoked by PTSD.

This ongoing exaggerated emotional response leads to all kinds of coping strategies, many of which are very unhealthy. If my grandmother hadn't offered me sherry when I was a child, I might not have started craving drink so soon, but I probably would have discovered it sooner or later on my own.

The atmosphere in some of the schools and classes I attended was an early, difficult, and traumatic experience for me, and for my parents too. Liscarroll has a gifted poet named Philip Egan who wrote a poem called "A Child's Prayer" about this. Here are a few lines:

Dear Holy God,
Please help me to be good at school
For when I get my homework wrong
The Teacher says that I'm a fool.
God, I've been crying all night long.

He slaps me with his stick and cane
And then he says that I am dumb,
Dear God, I cannot bear the pain;
My hands are black and blue and numb.

Why must the teacher, in a rage,
Hit us small boys who do not know
How best to write down on a page
The Gaelic words for frost and snow?

The repeated traumas of my military experience were layered on top of those school experiences. A good friend named Jonathan Tarr, a fellow army veteran whom I met that first night of college after my training at the institute, was a safe person to share with, and that relieved some of the pressure and horror of what I had seen. I was able to open up to Jonathan about my most painful memories from my time in the army.

◇⊷━◉ ◉━⊶◇

I was assigned to drive a quartermaster named Paddy Doyle through the mountains in Kosovo, on the border with Macedonia. It was a logistical assignment and I had different jobs to do and plenty of freedom. Paddy knew the country well because he had been there for a while, when things had been a lot worse.

The fighting was over, but the people were traumatized by the violent and bloody conflict that had resulted in ethnic cleansing. I saw mass graves and heard terrible stories. The people were hollow-eyed, their friends and family members all victims of genocide—and they were just trying to pick up the pieces and survive what had been done to them.

People in the villages were desperate, especially mothers of children.

One particular job was to take food to a Romani Gypsy compound with a chap named Tony. After we packed the food in the back of the Jeep, we set out. On the way, Tony advised me to keep an eye on my sidearm, a 9mm handgun. The compound was an old school with busted-out windows. It looked abandoned.

As soon as we pulled up, all of a sudden, heads started to appear in the window openings. Children started to spill out the door. Then men and women rushed outside.

"Throw out the food!" Tony said.

Before I knew it, we were engulfed by hundreds of hungry men, women, and children. For the first time in my life I saw what real hunger was. A grown man was beating a child for a loaf of bread. Mothers with babies in their arms were trying to grab something, anything. We were surrounded by chaos. I saw, smelled, and heard the poverty, the hunger. As we drove through the crowd, I couldn't get the image of that man hitting a young child out of my mind.

The Romani community were caught up in the war and treated horribly. The Serbs used them to target the Albanians, and when the war was over, the Albanians retaliated and targeted the gypsies. They were a minority caught in the middle.

Many refugees fled to Macedonia, and a large percentage of them were Romas. One weekend I went to St. Patrick's Irish Bar in Skopje, Macedonia, a bar I visited quite often. I had gotten to know the staff, and some of them invited me to go out with them after they finished work. I wasn't in uniform so being either brave or stupid, I decided it was okay and joined them.

After eating and having a few drinks, I was first out of the café. As I opened the door, I saw something at my feet. I thought it was a crumpled rag and was about to kick it away when I looked down and saw what it really was: a baby.

I immediately went into some kind of dream state, in shock and not at all able to process the sight of an abandoned child lying in front of the steps. I just stood and stared.

By the infant's tiny features I sensed that the baby was a girl, wrapped up in a blanket, only her face showing. It was freezing outside, and her skin was blue, her eyes closed. She wasn't moving.

"Come on, let's go," someone said, grabbing my arm and pulling at me.

I didn't resist. I was under orders, after all, and we were trained to suspect anything out of the ordinary as potentially dangerous. Maybe the mother was nearby watching, or maybe this was some kind of trap. What could I do anyway?

Here's the worst part about this story—none of this really impacted me until the birth of my Darragh. I stuffed the memory deep inside, along with any feelings, and didn't tell anyone or give it any thought. But one day baby Darragh got a cut on his forehead and we took him to the doctor for stitches. I was holding him in my arms when the doctor gave Darragh a shot to sedate him for the procedure, and as he went limp in my arms, I went into a flashback.

Immediately I was back on that street, on the edge of Macedonia, staring down at that little bundle. And for the first time, I felt something. I felt what I should have felt back then, but couldn't because my heart and soul had been too dark and dead. But now, my heart was coming alive again, with baby Darragh my lifeline, and the hopelessness and despair of that place, and that moment—it all came back to me in a flash.

I see the baby again. I am there.

Is she alive? I can't tell.

"Wait," I say. "What should we do?"

"Just go," the others say.

I stand, looking down, trying to decide what to do.

"Come on!" they say.

So I listen and I walk away.

I knew the baby had been laid on the doorstep by a desperate mother, in hopes that someone would save her child's life. I do not know if that little baby was still alive when I saw her, but I do know I left her there.

This is the worst, most painful memory of my life. In what universe do human beings find a helpless child in the freezing cold and just walk away?

I confessed and my friend Jonathan listened. His friendship and grace helped me to recall it, talk about it, and begin to recover.

I cannot go back and save that baby, but I can tell her story. She was precious, she was loved, she was made in the image of God, and yet she died a victim of a monstrous war. I will never forget her. May God forgive me for not picking her up, even if it had cost me everything.

Jonathan and I would sit and talk for hours, and that connection seemed to infuse light into the layers of darkness for both of us. He was one of the first people who made me feel safe and able to take off my emotional armor and expose my true feelings. He understood where I was coming from, and I could be real with him. Sadly, Jonathan died in 2019 while working in Sierra Leone, leaving behind his wife and children here in Ireland. I helped carry the coffin at his funeral. Though we were friends just seven years, I miss him and know he's here with me, looking over my shoulder and cheering me on.

One afternoon at home not long ago, I was playing on the floor with Odhrán. Eileen had bought a small watermelon at the market and Odhrán and I were laughing as he rolled it around. He picked it up a few inches and let it drop, which split open the bottom a bit. I picked the melon up before everything got messy and handed it to Eileen. She cut it open on the kitchen counter, and it was beautifully ripe, a rich red inside. Suddenly, I started feeling sick, then hot, then dizzy. I dropped to my knees, looked at Eileen, and said, "I need a minute."

I ran to the bathroom and was violently ill. It was a PTSD episode with no warning, triggered by the sight of the watermelon. Up till now, my episodes were usually brought on when I'd hear a helicopter flying overhead, but this time it was the red flesh of the watermelon that made my stomach turn, reminding me of things I'd seen that I can never unsee.

As I hunched over the toilet, sick and dizzy, my head spinning, I started crying. Then I felt four little hands on my back. It was Ellen-Rose and Odhrán. They'd come into the bathroom and were patting me on the back. Eileen was there too, her hand gently resting on my shoulder.

"Daddy, why are you crying?" asked Ellen-Rose, curious and concerned.

I don't know, I wanted to say. *I can't explain it. I'm not myself. I'm somewhere else, reliving things I wish I could forget. My traumas are scars on my soul like the one on my arm.*

I thought of Jonathan and how he experienced this too. He had cared and wanted me to heal, just like Eileen and the kids did now. I slowly left the past and was carried back to the present. I came out of it, but I was a wreck the rest of the day.

This is PTSD, and it's what almost killed me. It's why I want to help others who are facing the same struggle with their own inner shadows.

I was in the kitchen with Dad, having a cup of tea and a chat. He looked at me and said, "You showed 'em all, didn't you, Patrick?"

Those words were the closest he had ever come to saying he was proud of me. I don't think Dad knew his donkey sanctuary would end up saving me, too, but it did.

Life is much more precious to me now. Instead of feeling those almost irresistible urges to end my life, I thank God for each day with Eileen and the children. Several years ago, the old oak tree on the hill that was part of those dark fantasies rotted and fell down. Tim and I cut it up for firewood to warm our houses, the best use for it.

There is a new tree story I hold to now, with a tax collector named Zacchaeus. He was a short little man who wanted to see who Jesus was, but he was in a crowd of people and couldn't get a look. Then Zacchaeus had an idea. He ran ahead and climbed up a sycamore tree for a better view of Jesus, who was coming that way. When Jesus got to the tree, he stopped, looked up, and said, "Zacchaeus, get down. I'm coming to your house."

Zacchaeus quickly scrambled down and walked joyfully with Jesus back to his big house. Everyone was angry that Jesus was spending time with a greedy traitor like a tax collector. But the encounter transformed Zacchaeus. "I'll give half of everything to the poor, Jesus! And whoever I have cheated, I will pay back four times the amount!"

"Today you are saved, Zacchaeus," said Jesus. He embraced this lonely, awkward misfit, seeing him for who he really was— someone who needed to be seen and loved, and who needed hope and a new life. That was my story too.

I was like Jacksie—a baby starting over, needing care and nurturing to find my way again. Every time he hears my voice and starts in with his creaky braying, all I hear in my heart is the beautiful music of a creature who should have died but is very much alive and making a joyful noise. It's Jacksie's song.

Thanks to Jacksie and the other donkeys, I have a purpose—to use what has happened to me to help others.

CHAPTER EIGHTEEN

O COME YE HOME

Now sweetly lies old Ireland
Emerald green beyond the foam,
Awakening sweet memories,
Calling the heart back home.

IRISH PROVERB

LITTLE ELLEN-ROSE AND I were having a talk. She has rich blonde hair like my mam's that frames her face in soft curls. Her creamy fair skin with rosy cheeks complements her blue eyes, as blue as Mam's eyes, the color of the Irish Sea. She is an introspective, thoughtful little three-year-old full of questions.

"Daddy, what's it like to look out the window of the castle and see us over here?"

"Wow, Ellen. That is something I have to think about." I wonder what kind of answer she's looking for. Is she a daydreamer like me? Or does she have a spirit of adventure and want to climb the stone towers and see the world from up high? Maybe she's curious about what our family looks like from someone on the outside looking in.

I hold out my arms, and she comes in for a quick hug. She

hugs when she's ready, but not before. She's still recovering from the trauma of her little brother Odhrán's illness, and her Mam's too. She picks up a book and begins to flip the pages.

"Ellen-Rose, imagine you're in that window, up in the tower, and looking down here. What do you think you see?"

She looks up, her eyes bright. "Wow, Daddy. We're having fun."

"Yes, we are. And someday we'll climb up in the castle and look out the window! Now go get your shoes. We're going to Grandad's to see Jacksie."

I love that when she imagines looking out the window of Liscarroll Castle, she doesn't see battles or tiny buildings, but she sees us, our family, together and having fun.

"Eileen, I'm putting Odhrán's coat on him," I call into the kitchen. Odhrán is squirming, not wanting to put his arms into his coat, which is already getting small on him.

We pack up the picnic—ham and cheese sandwiches with tomato and mayonnaise (no Bovril, sadly), along with soda bread, crisps, bananas, and some chocolate. Water bottles and a flask of hot tea, and we're ready to go.

"Ellen-Rose, can you carry this?" I hand her a bag of old bread. "It's for the donkeys."

Ellen grabs the bag and runs out the front door and climbs into the car. I hold my hand out to Odhrán; he puts his small hand in mine, and I give it a little squeeze. We walk out to the car and I buckle him into his car seat.

Eileen comes out and hands me a backpack and gives me a smile. We're on lockdown for the COVID-19 virus, and we've never had this much time together at home with the kids and with each other before. There's been more time with Dad, too, and my sisters. The village has come back to life as well. People are out and about, taking walks and talking (with appropriate physical distancing, of course).

It's a strange season with its own fears and worries—all of us have been worried about Mam, who is in a care home nearby. She was diagnosed with Alzheimer's a few years ago and needs extra help these days. But the care home where she lives is close to the hills, full of light and friendly helpers, the residents in comfy chairs with handknit blankets. Through the windows you can see donkeys grazing in the fields.

Right now, with the pandemic, she's on a strict lockdown and we're not allowed inside. Even Dad can't see her, and that's very hard because Mam and Dad belong together. They're like a pair of deeply bonded donkeys who pine for each other when separated, but we know we'll be able to see her again soon. For now, she's safe inside.

When we arrive at Mam and Dad's house and pull into the driveway, Dad appears at the glass patio door with a smile on his face. He's holding a leash for Luna, his latest rescue dog. She's a little bit energetic, wiggling with joy, her tail wagging and knocking into the kids. Odhrán and Ellen-Rose give her a quick pat on the head and then race ahead to the gate of the sanctuary. Dad, Eileen, and I follow.

I look at Eileen. I can't believe we're here, in this moment, together. Dad opens the gate and we pile through, a messy little herd of humans. Just for fun I let out a low donkey call, just to say hello and let them all know we're coming. Somewhere in the distance I hear a screechy honking start up, like someone trying to blow through a partially blocked clarinet.

"Jacksie!" I call out. "How are ye?"

There's a full-throated bray in response this time, coming closer. I'm glad Jacksie's behind a fence, otherwise he'd be running up to me for a big wrestling and play biting session, tossing his head and braying and screeching all the way, frightening the kids. He still thinks he's human, although he's made friends with some of the other rescue donkeys and learned how to play the donkey way.

We're walking through the barns now, up the same walkways I took when I was a lad. Inside, I would watch Mam or Dad dressed in their work clothes and Wellies mix feed or chop vegetables for the donkeys. The sanctuary has undergone a massive transformation, greatly expanded to accommodate its growth. There are offices where Aran and Spot used to follow me to my grandmother's house. She has long since passed, and my Aunt Julia lives in the stone house now with her dog Rocky.

The old hen shed is an animal welfare department office. The lime tree I used to climb is now at the entrance to the Donkey Sanctuary, with a tidy parking lot for the 50,000 visitors who come every year to visit the historic farm, meet the donkeys, and climb the grassy steps on the trail up to the top.

We pass the barns and Aran's old stall. Good old Aran—he was adopted out, and while I lost track of him while I was in the army, I have a strong feeling he ended up in a good home with his new people. *I wonder if they let him in the house to watch TV?* The thought makes me laugh. A donkey who can open gates and doors keeps life interesting!

Ahead is a familiar straight grassy path with a very gentle climb, barely noticeable, with fences on both sides. To the right the hill slopes steeply upward, dotted with bushes and trees, with a herd of young donkeys about halfway up. They're eating and playing, ignoring us.

To the left are the big open grassy pastures, several of them, with a large herd of donkeys grazing, all different colors, shapes, and sizes. Each one has a loose plastic neck collar with a name on it. In the middle is a big oval patch of dirt, where I see Jacksie on his back, twisting and rolling in a cloud of dust. He catches sight of us and the kids cry out, "Jacksie!"

He rolls upright, puts his front legs out, then his back legs, his rear end goes up first and then his back and head. He shakes himself and jogs over to us, greeting us with a big bray and a shake of his head that scares Odhrán. He starts to whimper a bit, but Eileen picks him up, and he feels safe in her arms.

Sometimes I take the kids into the pasture with me and let the herd of donkeys surround us, greeting us with gentle sniffs and nibbles and whiskery touches on our backs and shoulders and hair. But not today—today it's Jacksie's turn.

"Daddy!" Odhrán cries, as I grab the top of the fence and vault over into the field, running toward Jacksie, then giving him a good fake. Right, then left, and him running behind me, nodding his head up and down, ready for a game.

We chase each other around the pasture, me always dodging him so he doesn't try to give me a hug, then we stop. I back up against his side and lean back, my arms stretched out across his back lengthwise, one arm pointing to his tail and one arm behind his neck, and Jacksie spins slowly. It's a little dance we came up with long ago, and we know the steps.

After a few turns, I give his withers a good scratch and jog back to my family, Jacksie trotting behind me like a puppy. I vault back over the fence, take Odhrán in my arms, and we start up the steep grassy steps to the rock. Jacksie bleats a complaint behind us, then quickly loses interest and goes back to his friends.

The wicket gate is gone and so is the big oak tree with the swings, where Eileen and I used to try to knock each other off. The ruins of the ring fort are up on the crown of the hill, sinking down into the earth and barely visible. Someone painted them white years ago and they look like a giant's bones or teeth.

We walk around the top of the hill on the circular path, looking across the rolling green hills stretched out around us, dotted with cattle and sheep, and crisscrossed with stone walls and hedges. There are cottages with thin wisps of smoke rising from some of the chimneys. About a quarter of the way around we look down and see the castle, still the star at the head of the village. Behind it stretches Main Street, lined with shops and homes, then the church and the school, and finally The Old Walls at the far end.

Our whole lives are within this sanctuary and in this village— every milestone, all of our successes and failures, our friends and family, our joys and sorrows. It used to frustrate me to be known so well and to live amidst a sea of traditions and expectations and ritual, but now it's starting to seem like a powerful web of inter-connectedness generation after generation, of people doing life together, trying to watch out for each other, raising the next gen-eration while taking care of the last, and working hard to preserve our culture and traditions.

I believe it's no accident that the Donkey Sanctuary is located here, in this place. As we walk around to the other side of the oval path at the top, we pass by the rock. I've always thought this was a sacred place. The rock is my anchor to the earth, the lookout stone where I could see into the past, tether myself to the present, and dream about the future.

In my mind's eye I see myself atop the rock as an innocent lad, a troubled teenager, a desperate young man, an alcoholic in recovery seeing everything with fresh eyes, and a newly married man with his bride. Odhrán, Ellen-Rose, Eileen, and I hop the fence and head to the rock, sitting there together and enjoying our picnic. We're making new memories.

Dad walks on with Luna, and I'm guessing he's remembering his own moments up here too, with his childhood donkey, Neddy, his parents and his brother, Mam, three daughters and a son, and now his grandchildren. And, of course, the donkeys. Always the donkeys.

For me, heaven and hell collided in this place, and it's my choice today, and every day, which field I will step into. For much of my life I was tempted to stray over into the fields of deceptively lush grass, only to find nothing came from them but sorrow, loss, and pain. Now I'm trying to learn how to cultivate the barren, stony field, watching things start to grow, and anticipating the time when I can appreciate the fruits of my labor and the rewards of being responsible.

This sanctuary and the rock are so very Irish, so steeped in history, every inch fought over, conquered, and reclaimed. It's a place full of mystery that whispers to the spirit in song and verse. I've always prided myself on being Irish and carrying our strong heritage and culture. If my island were a human being like me, I hope I would represent well our strengths and weakness, our love and compassion, our sense of humor and friendship, and our fierce bonds to family and village.

Having been raised a Catholic, I grew up feeling our way of faith was the only way. But during a recent meditation, I saw a big field full of rectangular wooden garden boxes, like the community vegetable and flower gardens you sometimes see in cities. The big raised wooden boxes represented the different faith communities in the world.

My box was the Catholic box, a mixture of fear, values, rituals, templates, love, and compassion, but above all, a judging God. I grew up with a constant fear of God, causing the nutrients in the box's soil to become contaminated and toxic, making it hard to grow anything other than weeds. As the weeds multiplied, the box broke and the bulbs and plants in the soil scattered out onto the field to wither and die.

I don't know much about the other kinds of boxes, but I'm learning that God is not tied to any one box. He is bigger than the boxes, and he is the master gardener who plants, and is ready to feed, tend, protect, and nourish if we ask him for help. He's near and patiently waiting for us to ask.

If I'm made in God's image as the Bible says, then he is the original donkey whisperer, and I am living out his dream for me by the work I've been doing and the work I will do. Since I am made in his image, my heart's desire is to project that image to the world today.

He is always there, and he doesn't care how long you've been away or how far you've strayed. I like to think he has a donkey something like Jacksie by his side, too, for companionship and a laugh.

I was fortunate to have the rich soil of Liscarroll, and the Donkey Sanctuary, to grow up in and to come back to when I was ready to find my soul and my soul's mission. The sanctuary is a microcosm of what the world could be like if we lived in harmony with nature and each other, like the donkeys do, under the canopy of heaven with the rock, our Lord, at the center.

After we finish our picnic, we head down the hill with the donkeys watching us from the fields or walking alongside us. The kids are tired, and after we say goodbye to Dad and make sure he has something for dinner, I drop Eileen and the kids off at home so I can go and visit Mam.

The care home is on lockdown so I can't go inside, but we can talk through the window. I call and Mam's caregivers bring her up to the window; she's at a point where she's not even sure what a window is anymore. She thinks if she sees you through the clear glass, she can reach right through it.

I look at her straight blonde hair, the color of Irish butter, and her clear blue eyes. I put up my hand for a wave, and she responds by reaching her hand out as if she wants to hold my hand.

I place my palm against the window, and she puts her hand

against my palm on her side. I can almost feel it . . . almost. She looks thinner now, and I wonder if she knows me or remembers my name.

She looks up at me then, and her eyes light up. She knows me!

I blow her a kiss and she tries to return it, but she can't quite figure out how to do it. I love that she's trying, and if I don't get anything else today, on my birthday, I'll take this effort at a kiss and a clasped hand from Mam as the only birthday gift I need.

A flash of memory comes to me—another window reflecting a broken man full of shadows who almost died trying to break out of himself. My mam was there too, in that moment, holding my hand when I needed her most.

One last kiss to Mam through the window as her caregivers come and I say goodbye. On the short drive home, I think again about my new eyes and how there was so much beauty and richness and love all around me my entire life, and I couldn't see it. Now I can see it, even through a glass with Mam, and I'm so grateful.

When I pull into the driveway at our house, I stop the car and glance at the front door. I can see Eileen through the glass, playing with the kids on the floor. I sit in the car for a minute, reveling in a happy dream. *Is this my life?* I never thought this could happen, and it did. I don't have to feel alone, or lonely, or like I don't belong anymore. And on my good days, I don't.

On my bad days, I add this to my morning ritual. I put my hands out, palms up, in front of me, and whatever is worrying me, angering me, plaguing me, or weighing me down, I place on my open palms. Then I envision laying those things on the altar and giving them to God. I mostly do it in the mornings, offering up my problems inside the house at my morning prayer and meditation time, but if needed, I can do it anywhere, at any time. When I feel the darkness rising, I offer everything to God, and the shadows melt back down and slip away.

I'm a proud son of beautiful Ireland, but it's hurting with a generation far removed from faith, lost and in so much pain. I know where they are, and where they have been, because I've been there, too. My story has had more dark days than bright days, but I want to be like Marie—to really see people, to know them, to care about them, and to help them with their healing and growth.

I was lucky, or maybe I was blessed, to find a way out. I want to make my mother proud of me for being someone who works hard, takes care of his family, remembers what he's been taught, and rescues those put in his path who need help, whether human or animal.

Once upon a time, a lad from the village stood on the rock and looked down at the castle, dreaming about joining the battle. But he had to learn he wasn't strong enough to fight the battle alone. He needed help. One day he stopped running, called out, and help came.

That help has never stopped. He decided to try to help others with the help he'd been given, and to share what he learned from the donkeys.

And they all lived happily ever after . . . especially Jacksie!

ΛFTERWORD

My son, Patrick, was brought up on a rural farm in the southwest of Ireland where there were cattle, horses, donkeys, and mules. As he had no brother to play with, his brothers were the animals, and he spent his days playing in the fields. The donkeys were to become a big part of his life and ours, too, of course.

In 1964 donkeys began arriving on our farm after being rescued by my father, Garrett Barrett, who served as an inspector for the Irish Society for Prevention of Cruelty to Animals (ISPCA). In 1981 I went out on call with my dad for the first time, and the very last time. The report out of County Kerry indicated a bad cruelty case, with horses and bullocks in a dreadful condition, their heads having been tethered to their legs. My father's job was to cut them free from their bonds with a Stanley knife. He had about twenty of them freed when he suddenly beckoned to me to help. As he handed me the knife, he dropped dead on the ground from a massive heart attack. I was thirty-four years old.

I followed the ambulance carrying my father, accompanied by the head of the ISPCA, a woman named Miss Turketine. In the car, I turned to her and said, "I will do my father's work." It was

December 1981, and my destiny was decided in that cold, bleak field. Within a month, I took over Dad's job. Patrick was two and a half at the time, and along with his older sisters Helen, Debbie, and Eileen, and my wife, Eileen, our lives became firmly rooted in caring for neglected animals.

There were already thirty-two rescue donkeys on the family farm in Liscarroll. At the time, donkeys were being made redundant as farm machinery was taking over their once honorable jobs. Donkeys are such strong and stoic animals, and they live well into their fifties. Increasingly, donkeys were abandoned in fields and on roadsides, left to the mercy of the relentless Irish weather. The situation was becoming dire.

In 1987, the Donkey Restfield Ireland, which our home place had first been named, affiliated with The Donkey Sanctuary in England. The Donkey Sanctuary Ireland was established, and I was the founder. More than six thousand donkeys have been rescued from all over the island of Ireland, with my wife, Eileen, working by my side.

Patrick worked here in the early years after school. The donkeys were his playful friends, but I always had to make sure he was safe because he would march into the grazing herds as brave as can be. Some donkeys had different temperaments and could be overly frisky, but Patrick never seemed to have any fear of them and was always very kind in his handling of them, even as a young boy.

It was no surprise that Patrick joined the army at the age of nineteen, given his desire for adventure and his will to help others. He would phone most weeks to let us know he was safe because he knew what a worrier I was. After he left the army, Patrick came back to work here. I noticed he was different than before he went away, but he never spoke much about his experiences. At the time I took it that he was stressed out after all he had been through and witnessed. He would head off and be gone all night, and I would wait up for him to come in safe. Many nights I prayed the Rosary that he would return home. I would hold my Padre Pio medal and pray for his protection.

The day finally arrived when Patrick had to enter a treatment center. Eileen was the stoic strong one, while I spent the whole time praying, pacing, drinking strong tea, and hoping for his recovery.

Afterward, I could see a great change for the better. Patrick began studying counseling and psychology to help people in a similar position to himself. Since his qualification he has grown from strength to strength. I see a lot of the freedom in him now that he had as a young boy running through the fields.

Patrick and his family call regularly, and I love our chats over a warm cup of tea, reminiscing of all that has gone by and of what is yet to come. I often stand at the kitchen door and watch him head off for his walk in the sanctuary and I feel a swell of pride for the man he has become. I often walk with him, my Rosary beads in my hand, feeling grateful, feeling proud, feeling happy. My son has come home.

Paddy Barrett, founder of The Donkey Sanctuary Ireland

Patrick Barrett
and his herds

I am blessed to be surrounded by both people

and donkeys—the family in Ireland I love.

It's time for you to meet them! Here's a roundup of

selected photographs—past and present—that capture

a wee bit of my life and story.

My grandmother Eileen as a girl in London,
walking her father's beloved Scottie dogs.

◄ 1968:
Mam and Dad's
wedding day
in London.

The Donkey Sanctuary in the early days.

Mam, always having a gentle
touch with the donkeys.

"I grew up on the back
of a donkey . . ." ▶

Aran was a forgotten donkey
on a lonely island, his feet
in terrible shape. He soon
became my best friend. ▼

◀ Guinness and me
next to the Rock.

◄ A village girl named Eileen on a neighbor's derby (racing) donkey. Our paths would cross again.

My sister Eileen (9) trying to push me (7) off the bonnet of the car, all in good fun. ►

Helen, Mam, and me with a lovely American lady who visited every year after reading about Dad's work in *National Geographic*.

◀ My sister Helen (19) in the middle of the herd.

Me posing like a tough soldier on the border of Israel and Lebanon.

The view from the Sanctuary. Amid the nightmare
of war, this is where I lived in my head.

Entryway to Liscarroll Castle.

◄ Praying at St. Mary's in Mallow, where I begged God to save my boys' lives.

At the cross with Eileen on Carrauntoohil, the highest point in Ireland. ►

Marrying Eileen . . .
my *anam cara*,
my soul mate. ▶

On the Rock with my
family: Eileen,
Daragh, Darragh, and
Patrick. ▶

Jacksie going in for his daily roll.

◄ Jacksie saying,
"Come in and play."

Jacksie having a cuddle. ►

Jacksie breathing me in, his whole body smiling.

▲ Sanctuary at last.

◄ The Olde Fiddle,
the place where
I took my last drink
on a morning that changed
my entire life.

◄ With my dad at the top of the Rock, our special place.

A new generation at the sanctuary. Little Darragh (4) with my dad. ►

My family—my "herd"—today, including our two youngest, Ellen-Rose and Odhrán.

Acknowledgments

PATRICK BARRETT

To Susy: Who would have thought that sending an email in faith would have led us here? Thank you for your extreme patience, tolerance, and wonderful ability to bring this story to life. You have been a great mentor and teacher for me. God bless you and your family—friends of ours forever.

To Sarah Atkinson and Bonne Steffen: I really enjoyed working with both of you and the entire Tyndale team. It was a privilege. Thank you for believing that a man and his donkeys were worth hearing.

To the village of Liscarroll: The friendships, laughs, and stories that we have shared have made me the man I am today. A piece of the village is forever framed in my heart, reminding me to blossom where I am planted. A special thank-you to Philip Egan for your poetry and advice. And to Pat O'Brien for letting us experience the history of Liscarroll village through your eyes.

To my childhood friends whom I shared so many scrapes and adventures with: Sean Murphy, Brian Brosnan, Barry Madden, Brendan O'Connor, and Roy Gardiner.

To Flatstone Counselling & Psychotherapy Institute and their team: Dónal Healy (RIP) and Clare Murray for having the vision to create an institute that would become a healing and educational environment for all. You really did believe in me and push me over the line! To Marie Stuart for "seeing me" on the 24th of November 2012. To Anne Paffrey for seeing my true colours and encouraging me to train as a psychotherapist. To Helen O'Dea for always listening to me. And to Alan Davis for your support and words of wisdom throughout.

To all my Flatstone colleagues: Nuala, Liam, Sharon, and Jacinta. I have no doubt that your healing light is shining in many lives. To Martina Brett and family—you are my family. Thank you for your friendship always.

To The Irish Defence Forces and all the people I served with. It was an honour and an experience.

To my dear friend Jonathan Tarr (RIP): We shared our hearts, souls, and experiences. I know you are with me always, bud.

A heartfelt thank-you to Noreen, Jackie, the Healy family, and my brothers-in-law. For the warm welcome and warm dinners! And for supporting Eileen and me on our journey together.

A thank-you to the McCormack and Barrett clans. I am proud to be a member of both tribes.

To my three sisters—Debbie, Helen, and Eileen—a very special thank-you. You have put up with a lot from me! Thank you for all your care and support throughout my life. You always took care of me and put me on the right path. I am not sure if I would have found that path without you all. To your husbands—Tim, John, and Timmy—you have a lot to put up with too!

Mom and Dad: The Sanctuary you both built is a lasting legacy to your devotion, care, and love of the donkey. That same devotion, care, and love you poured on your children. *Thank you* is not a big enough word for all you did for me through the good times and bad.

To my own treasures: Odhrán for your character, joy, and spirit in our home. You never fail to make us laugh! To my beautiful little girl, Ellen-Rose. Your strength, determination, and softness are an inspiration. Patrick, your care for animals is who you are. Thank you for your thoughtfulness, fun, and kindness. Darragh, my firstborn—I have learned so much from you. You have incredible strength, honesty, and humour! "Big" Daragh: Thank you for bringing music and creativity into our home. Your laughter and joy are missed while you're studying abroad. Daisy, our dog—for just being you! I am truly blessed to have you. I love you all deeply and forever.

To my beautiful wife and soulmate, Eileen: "Happiness is when what you think, what you say, and what you do are in harmony." You are my happiness.

To the donkeys: You've provided me with a life and a sanctuary to grow up in. Thank you for teaching me the truest values—loyalty, honesty, friendship, and love.

And a special thank-you to Jacksie: You mad donkey!

SUSY FLORY

To Jan Harris, Sarah Atkinson, Bonne Steffen, and the whole wonderful team at Tyndale, a hearty thank-you for embracing this unique story. Your books and your work are making a profound difference in this world.

A heartfelt thanks to Marci Seither and Keri Wyatt Kent for going to Ireland with me, exploring ruined castles and monasteries, cooking lovely dinners back at the log cabin, and for falling in love with Patrick, his family, and his story as much as I did. You are amazing friends.

My love and thanks to Lorena Bathey, Kathi Lipp, Cheri Gregory, Michele Cushatt, Jeanette Hanscome, the WCCW Team, Jennifer Grant and INK, the Gertie Girls, Debbie Warren, Joel Pincosy, and so many other writer friends, too many to count, who have been praying for me and cheering on this book. A special thank-you to all of my memoir-writing friends at Everything Memoir, who have loved this story and been interested from the very first time I posted some Jacksie photos in the group.

A very special thank-you to my prayer team, formed for my second trip to Ireland: Carole Taylor, Cheryl Thompson, Eileen Grafton, Uncle Jim Serna, Laura Christianson, and Rita Hassna. Thank you for having my back.

Patrick, may you be blessed for opening your heart and spirit and sharing your story with me, and now with the world; thank you for trusting me with your story. You have taught me so much about trusting God and listening to his voice. To Eileen, for the wisdom, humor, and friendship; I'm sorry my arm ruined our dinner out, and next time I'm there, please let's have a redo! The Healys, for opening your kitchen to me, and Noreen for the scones, tea, and a mother's touch. Paddy-One, for your wisdom and kindness. You are a hero for saving so many donkeys, and people, over the years. Thanks for showing me the Padre Pio medal. To Patrick's mam, Eileen, I'm so glad I got to meet you and enjoy your beauty and your smile. Helen, thank you for telling me your stories and for all you do for animals and people. And Jacksie, I love you for being full of life, mischief, and joy, and for being an ambassador at the Donkey Sanctuary.

Thank you, Philip Egan, for welcoming me to your beautiful pub, giving me a book of your poetry, and sharing your gift of words, memories, and wisdom with us. You are a treasure. Thank you, Pat O'Brien, for carrying the stories of past generations, both the heroes and the villains, and for stewarding the castle. I'll never forget the day you showed us around.

A thank-you to Steve Laube, best agent ever, for "getting" this story from the very first time I told you about it. I appreciate your wisdom and encouragement.

Last, a deep thank-you to my own herd: Robert, Ethan, Angela, Teddy, and Forrest, for caring about me and my writing and for listening to the stories and sharing your thoughts and ideas. I'm also thinking of my mom, Mary Jane Daugherty Srubar, and how much she loved Ireland and storytelling. She was very proud of being a daughter of Ireland and considered herself an Irish princess. Her first and only trip to Ireland in 2001 was a dream come true for her. This one is for you, Mum!

About the Donkey Sanctuary

At the Donkey Sanctuary Ireland, many thousands of neglected or abandoned donkeys like Aran and Jacksie are still being saved, even though Dad retired a few years ago. He was awarded a place in the National Hall of Fame, a high honor in Ireland, in recognition for his contribution to animal welfare. The ceremony was a large gala held at a hotel up in County West Mead. The Donkey Breed Society presented the award. Dad gave a speech and said he wouldn't be receiving the award if it wasn't for his wife and family. I'll never forget that night, and I was so proud of my father and his career characterized by unselfish service to an animal that has so often been overlooked or mistreated. Like Marie, he saw what needed to be done, and he did it.

There is new leadership in place, and the Donkey Sanctuary continues the good work of rescuing donkeys. Visitors are welcome, with both admission and parking free.

The Donkey Sanctuary is located in the village of Liscarroll, Mallow, County Cork, Ireland. For more information, you can phone them at +353 (0) 22 48398 or visit them online at https://www.thedonkeysanctuary.ie/.

About PTSD

Post-traumatic stress disorder (PTSD) can develop after a very stressful or distressing event. It can also develop after a prolonged traumatic experience.

It isn't fully understood why some people develop the condition while others don't. But certain factors appear to make some people more likely to develop PTSD.

One possibility is that PTSD is there to help you survive further traumatic experiences. For example, the flashbacks you have with a PTSD experience may force you to think about the event in detail. This is supposed to make you better prepared if it happens again. The feeling of being "on edge" (hyperarousal) may develop to help you react quickly in another crisis.

While these responses may be intended to help you survive, they're actually unhelpful. They make it so you can't process and move on from the traumatic experience.

In most cases, the symptoms develop during the first month after a traumatic event. In a minority of cases, there may be a delay of months or even years before symptoms start to appear.

Some people with PTSD experience long periods when their symptoms are less noticeable. This is followed by periods where they get worse. Other people have constant, severe symptoms.

The specific symptoms of PTSD can vary among individuals. Symptoms generally fall into three categories:

- reexperiencing
- avoidance and emotional numbing
- hyperarousal (feeling "on edge")

Reexperiencing is the most typical symptom of PTSD. This is when you involuntarily and clearly relive the traumatic event in the form of:

- flashbacks
- nightmares
- repetitive and distressing images or sensations
- physical sensations such as pain, sweating, nausea, or trembling

You may have constant negative thoughts about your experience. You may repeatedly ask yourself questions that prevent you from coming to terms with the event. For example, you may wonder why the event happened to you and if you could have done anything to stop it. This can lead to feelings of guilt or shame.

The symptoms of complex PTSD are similar to symptoms of PTSD. They may include:

- feelings of shame or guilt
- difficulty controlling your emotions
- periods of losing attention and concentration—this is known as dissociation

- physical symptoms—such as headaches, dizziness, chest pains, and stomachaches
- cutting yourself off from friends and family
- relationship difficulties
- destructive or risky behavior such as self-harm, alcohol misuse, or drug abuse
- suicidal thoughts

The main treatments for PTSD are psychological therapies and medication.

Traumatic events can be very difficult to come to terms with, but confronting your feelings and seeking professional help is the recommended method for treating PTSD.

It's possible to treat PTSD many years after the traumatic event occurred. This means it's never too late to seek help.

NOTE: This helpful information is provided by the HSE, or The Health Service Executive (HSE), a government agency responsible for the provision of health and personal social services for everyone living in Ireland. https://www2.hse.ie/conditions /mental-health/post-traumatic-stress-disorder/post-traumatic-stress-disorder-ptsd -symptoms.html

ΛBOUΤ ΤΗΕ ΛUΤΗORS

PATRICK BARRETT grew up in Liscarroll, a small Irish village in Cork County, Ireland, where his parents founded Ireland's Donkey Sanctuary. As a teenager, Patrick joined the Irish Defence Forces and served in Kosovo and Lebanon from 1998 to 2003, then worked at the Donkey Sanctuary for almost a decade. It was during this period that his life turned around and The Donkey Sanctuary became a place of refuge where Patrick made strong reconnections to nature, the land, his family, God, and the wisdom of the donkeys. He became a psychotherapist in 2016 and uses what he learned at the sanctuary in his work with men suffering from PTSD and addiction. In 2015, Patrick married his childhood sweetheart, Eileen, and together they have five children.

SUSY FLORY is the *New York Times* bestselling author or coauthor of sixteen books, including *Thunder Dog: The True Story of a Blind Man, His Guide Dog, and the Triumph of Trust at Ground Zero*. Her book *The Unbreakable Boy*, written with Scott LeRette, is in production at Kingdom Story Company and Lionsgate Studios. Susy directs West Coast Christian Writers, a nonprofit that hosts writers conferences, and she is currently pursuing a master's degree in New Testament at Northern Seminary. Susy and her husband, Robert, have two adult children and live in the mountains of California.

Introducing Jacksie to my coauthor, Susy,
who helped bring this book to life.

A heartwarming true story of
LOYALTY, KINDNESS & HEALING,
Joey is a profound testament to the power of blind faith.

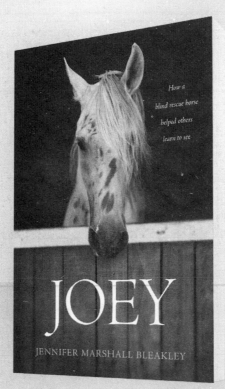

When a struggling ranch owner dedicated to helping troubled kids rescues a blind horse named Joey, the result is a story of friendship, faith, and overcoming. *Joey* will touch your heart and reveal the power of finding light in the darkest of places.